Supply Chain Manag
– in Theory and Pra

D0198709

Birgit Dam Jespersen & Tage Skjøtt-Larsen

Supply Chain Management
– in Theory and Practice

Copenhagen Business School Press

Supply Chain Management – in Theory and Practice

© Copenhagen Business School Press
Printed in Denmark by Holbæk Amts Bogtrykkeri
Cover design by Morten Højmark
1. edition, 2. impression 2006

ISBN 87-630-0152-7

Distribution:

Scandinavia
DJØF/DBK, Mimersvej 4
DK-4600 Køge, Denmark
Phone: +45 3269 7788, fax: +45 3269 7789

North America
Copenhagen Business School Press
Books International Inc.
P.O. Box 605
Herndon, VA 20172-0605, USA
Phone: +1 703 661 1500, fax: +1 703 661 1501

Rest of the World
Marston Book Services, P.O. Box 269
Abingdon, Oxfordshire, OX14 4YN, UK
Phone: +44 (0) 1235 465500, fax: +44 (0) 1235 465555
E-mail Direct Customers: direct.order@marston.co.uk
E-mail Booksellers: trade.order@marston.co.uk

Table of Contents

Preface

The competition has moved from competition between firms to competition between supply chains. Any company is linked to other organisations, whether it is suppliers, customers, third-party logistics providers, or intermediaries. The performance of the individual firm is therefore dependent on the strengths and weaknesses of its partners in the supply chain. As Charles Fine has expressed it in his seminal book "Clockspeed" from 1998: *"A company is its chain of continually evolving capabilities – that is, its own capabilities plus the capabilities of everyone it does business with".*

Supply Chain Management (SCM) has developed as a management concept during the last two decades and today many international companies have implemented the concept in their organisation. Notable examples are Cisco, Dell Computers, Gillette, Nike, Nokia, Procter & Gamble, and Zara.

In this book, we try to combine theoretical knowledge from international research with practical experiences in implementing and using the concept in companies. We have aimed to give a varied picture of SCM, including both positive and negative aspects. The book has a European perspective on SCM and most cases and illustrating examples are taken from European companies.

The book is intended for B.com, MSc, and MBA students on logistics and SCM courses. Besides, we hope that logistics managers and SCM professionals will find inspiration and guidelines for implementing SCM in their own organisation.

We want to express our gratitude to the companies, which have allowed us to use them as illustrating cases. We are also grateful to business process manager, Camilla Fink, Corporate Supply Chain, Carlsberg A/S, who has written a major part of chapter 5, including the Carlsberg Case, and logistics manager Per Thomsen and project manager Helene Kyvsgaard, both Sanistaal A/S, who have contributed with the Sanistaal Case.

Copenhagen, February 2005

Birgit Dam Jespersen   Tage Skjøtt-Larsen

1. Supply Chain Management – in Theory and Practice

Background

The competitiveness of international companies is highly dependent on their ability to deliver customised products quickly and timely all over the world. Therefore, focus has moved from competition between firms at the same level in the production process to competition between supply chains, from raw materials to end customers. A company's ability to create trust-based and long-term business relationships with customers, suppliers, and other strategic partners becomes a crucial competitive parameter. The tendency towards increased integration and cooperation between the enterprises in the supply chain results in greater complexity in the management and control technology, which requires increased coordination of resources and activities.

Most companies compete in an environment characterised by:
- Turbulent and dynamic markets, where the customers' requirements change rapidly and unforeseeably.
- Strongly segmented markets, where various customers have varying requirements for products and services.
- Market requirements for multiple product varieties and customisation of both products and services.
- Increasing customer demand for "experiences," and not merely physical products.
- Global competition, which forces companies to become faster, better, and cheaper.

These are the challenges that have made SCM an important management tool and competitive parameter for many firms.

Growing Interest in SCM

Supply Chain Management (SCM) is a management concept that can help a business get an overview of and manage cooperation in the supply chain based on a holistic view. In the past decade large international corporations such as Cisco, Dell Computer, Gillette, Kodak, LEGO, Motorola, Novozymes, Sony, 3M, Unilever, Xerox, and Wal-Mart have implemented SCM. Moreover, international consultancy firms such as IBM Business Consulting Services, A.T. Kearney, Cap Gemini, Ernst & Young, Accenture, and KPMG have adopted SCM as an important business area. A large number of universities and business schools, including the Cranfield School of Management, the Copenhagen Business School, Erasmus University, and the University of Cologne, have included SCM courses in their curricula.

Purpose and Scope

The purpose of this book is to:
- Provide an overview of the content and meaning of the SCM concept
- Demonstrate how SCM can be used to create competitive advantage
- Assess potentials, limitations, and risks related to SCM
- Provide management with general guidelines for central issues that should be considered and settled prior to implementation of the SCM concept

SCM is a very broad management concept. Consequently, it is not possible to treat all aspects within the framework set for this introductory book. Instead, focus is placed on the strategic and organisational opportunities and challenges presented by the SCM concept. This means that the more tactical/operative decisions related to day-to-day operations and maintenance of supply chain relationships are not dealt with here.

Nor is the intention to review concrete techniques or tools used for analysis of materials and product flows in supply chains. Standard textbooks on operations management may be referred to, e.g. Chopra & Meindl 2004, Simchi-Levi et al. 2003 and Slack et al. 2004.

What is SCM?

When new concepts are launched, there is always a great deal of confusion about definitions, content, and fields of application. Definitions from the literature on SCM serve to demonstrate the wide spectrum of what is understood as the concept of SCM.

Handfield & Nichols (2002) define **Supply Chain** and **Supply Chain Management** as follows:

> *The **Supply Chain** encompasses all organizations and activities associated with the flow and transformation of goods from the raw materials stage, through to the end user, as well as the associated information flows. Material and information flows both up and down the supply chain. **Supply chain management (SCM)** is the integration and management of supply chain organizations and activities through cooperative organizational relationships, effective business processes, and high levels of information sharing to create high-performing value systems that provide member organizations a sustainable competitive advantage.*

Christopher (2005) defines SCM as:

> *The management of upstream and downstream relationships with suppliers and customers to deliver superior customer value at less cost to the supply chain as a whole.*

This definition of SCM focuses on management of relationships as a means of achieving better results for all members of the supply chain, including customers. Christopher also claims that the term *supply chain management* is actually mismanaging. *Demand chain management* would be a better term and would stress the fact that the chain is driven by market forces and not by the supply side. Christopher further suggests that the word *chain* be replaced by *network*, because the supply chain is normally comprised of a complex network of players on both the vendor and the customer sides. In addition, the business' suppliers may often be customers and competitors in other scenarios.

According to the Council of Supply Chain Management Professionals (CSCMP),

> *SCM encompasses the planning and management of all activities involved in sourcing and procurement, conversion, and all Logistics Management activities. Importantly, it also includes coordination and collaboration with channel partners, which can be suppliers, intermediaries, third-party service providers, and customers.*[1]

Cooper, Lambert & Pagh (1997) define SCM as:

> *The integration of business processes from end user through original suppliers that provides products, services and information that add value for customers.*

This definition stresses the need for a broader understanding of the process concept, covering more than just the processes directly linked to the product and information flows.

The definition used in this book is very close to the last definition presented above, because there is a large, untapped potential in systematising all relevant processes across the businesses in the supply chain, and not just the logistics process. Our definition of SCM is then as follows:

> *SCM is the management of relations and integrated business processes across the supply chain that produces products, services and information that add value for the end customer.*

This definition contains several keywords. The first is *relations*, which is used here as the term for all activities linked with establishing, maintaining, and developing business relations with supply chain partners. The next keyword is *integrated*, defined as coordination across functional lines and legal corporate boundaries. The coordination may be organisational, for instance, in the form of cross-organisational teams and interfaces at many levels; system related, for instance, in the form of integrated information and communications systems, and EDI/Internet connections; or planning related, for instance, in the form of exchange of order data, inventory status, sales forecasts, production plans, and sales and marketing campaigns.

Business processes is the third keyword, which, for the purpose of this book, is limited to the processes that are directly related to the

---

[1] Former Council of Logistics Management, www.cscmp.org

production of products, services, and information. Examples of business processes are Order Fulfilment, Customer Service, Product Development, and Materials Supply. Other processes related, for example, to HRM, Risk Management, or finance, are not encompassed by the definition.

Use of the SCM concept entails that the links in the supply chain plan and coordinate their processes and relationships by weighing the overall efficiency and competitive power of the supply chain. Figure 1 shows a simple model of the overall supply chain.

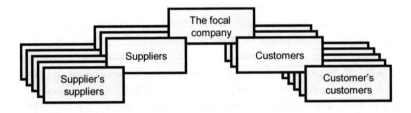

Figure 1.1 Example of a supply chain

As shown in Figure 1.1 there are a number of players involved in the overall supply chain, ranging from the raw materials vendor to the end customer. Each player contributes to the attainment of the overall goal. The overall goal for a supply chain is to fulfil the end customers' needs and expectations in a cost-efficient manner. This overall goal can be broken down into a range of more operational sub-goals, such as order cycle time, production lead time, rate of turnover, punctuality of delivery, and product availability. Many of these sub-goals may also contain more qualitative goals such as product development, customisation, market flexibility, environmental considerations, and product quality. Cost reductions are obtained through better coordination and planning, more knowledge of customers' and suppliers' needs and planning systems, as well as quick and open access to relevant planning data such as sales forecasts, current sales figures, production plans, and inventory status.

What is the Difference between Logistics and SCM?

SCM has grown out of the logistics concept but is distinct from this concept in several ways. Logistics is typically based on the individual business with the objective of making this enterprise's logistics system more efficient through internal and external planning and control. SCM is based on the external relationships between the players in the entire supply chain and focuses on how to improve trading in general. The SCM concept thus provides a broader perspective across the supply chain than has been the traditional approach within logistics. A range of activities comprised by the SCM concept concern expansion of the Business Process Reengineering (BPR) concept to cover the entire supply chain, as it is presupposed that the internal logistics has already become more efficient through BPR projects or the like.

Processes across the supply chain and the development of supply chain relationships are characteristics of SCM. Focus is on strengthening the overall supply chain rather than on sub-optimisation in the individual enterprise. A link in the chain may, for example, incur extra costs in the form of excess inventories of semi-manufactures, in order to bring down the total costs of the supply chain as a whole. This is typically seen in connection with just-in-time production, where the assembly plant can often benefit from postponing the procurement of components until the time when the specific customer order is placed. This presupposes that the component suppliers have larger inventories, so that they can handle fluctuations in demand.

In practice, businesses in a supply chain do not have integrated cooperation with all other players in the supply chain. Cooperation will often begin with dyadic relationships between the business and its key vendors and customers. Rarely is supplier cooperation expanded to include the vendor's suppliers or the customer's customers. It is usually left to the suppliers and customers to handle these relationships. But this does not preclude seeing the entire supply chain from an SCM perspective. Within the automobile industry there is often hierarchic vendor cooperation, where the automobile manufacturer cooperates with a number of system suppliers, each of which is responsible for cooperating with a number of component suppliers, which in turn are responsible for cooperating with vendors of sub-components and raw materials. This is illustrated in Figure 1.2.

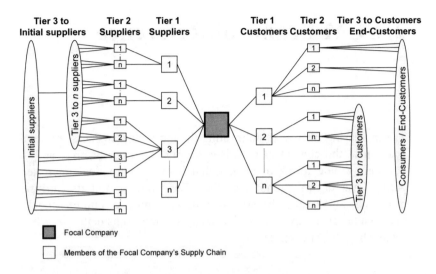

Figure 1.2 An example of a tier-structured Supply Chain

In many supply chains, the roles are not clearly defined. A supplier of components to an Own Equipment Manufacturer (OEM) might at the same time be a competitor to the OEM customer and marketing its own products to the OEM customer's customers. This is the case with Intel, which supplies processors to PC manufacturers and at the same time promotes its own products heavily to the end customers. A buying firm can also be supplier to its competitors. For example, in the car manufacturing industry engines from one car manufacturer are often used in competitors' cars.

2. SCM Frame of Reference

The increasing interest in delineating the individual business' roll and position in the context of a holistic supply chain perspective, and in developing new forms of cooperation between individual interested parties, has drawn attention to the SCM concept and its intrinsic principles. SCM can be broken down into a number of building blocks that make clear the need for analysis and consideration when establishing SCM cooperation.

Three Components in the SCM Concept

SCM can be divided into three components, which are tightly interconnected:
- Network structure
- Business processes
- Management

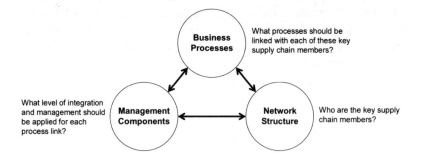

Figure 2.1 Components in the SCM concept
Source: Lambert, Cooper and Pagh (1998)

Network structure

The *Network* structure comprises the most important collaboration partners in a supply chain, as well as the relationships between these players. It is neither possible nor desirable to establish a SCM cooperative network that includes all participants in a business network.

It would demand entirely too many resources and be quite complex. Moreover, it is important to focus available resources on the relations that are of strategic importance for the competitiveness of the business. As a corollary to this reasoning, upper management must first consider the best choices for the cooperative partners of the business. In relation to the other active players in the supply chain, the business can adopt more traditional forms of cooperation, but it would be natural to transfer experience from the strategic cooperative partners where relevant.

For many businesses, it is a novel challenge to choose and work in a structured manner with business relationships. A good way to start is to describe the roles the business fills today, and the roles the business wishes to fill in the future in terms of the supply chain. In this way, it becomes possible to create a dialogue concerning which relationships must be developed in the future. Working towards creating and maintaining the right relationships becomes part of the business strategy.

In order to support this process, business relations can be put in general categories. Lambert (1998) suggests dividing relations into four main categories.

1. Relationships that the business in focus wishes to lead and coordinate. For a final assembly factory, a typical example would be relations to systems suppliers and customers in the next link of the supply chain.
2. Relationships that are non-critical for the business in focus, but which still should be monitored in order to ensure that the activities are completed satisfactorily by the other businesses involved in the network. Examples may include transport and storage/warehouse tasks that are contracted out to a third party.
3. Relationships that the business in focus does not deem to be critical or worth sacrificing management or monitoring resources on. For example, purchasing of standard goods, which can be purchased on short notice from several different vendors.
4. Relationships to other supply chains. A business can simultaneously be a supplier for several internally competing supply chains. These relationships are not viewed as part of the relationships in the actual supply chain, but can, of course, have an important influence on the supply chain's effectiveness and competitiveness. It is often suggested that suppliers deliver to competitors, in order to avoid becoming too dependent on one customer, and to ensure that the supplier remains competitive and innovative.

Business processes

Business processes encompass the activities and flows of information that are connected with conducting materials, products, and services through the supply chain and on to customers. Examples of some important business processes:

- Order processing
- Customer service
- Distribution
- Product development / Time-to-market
- Supply

The question of how many and which processes exist is of critical importance. Therefore the coordination of processes and integration of them in businesses is of great value. The quantity and specificity of processes of magnitude will vary from supply chain to supply chain. As a result, the choice of which processes are to be in focus, as well as the level and depth of integration in a given supply chain, is of great consequence.

Order processing

This business process includes all of the activities that are tied in with expediting customers' orders: the placement of the order, including transmission, the receiving of the order, as well as the credit check, the actual expedition of the order, the distribution, and finally, the customer receiving the order and invoicing. The total time that passes between when the customer places their order until the customer receives the desired goods is often referred to as the order cycle. Order placement, order confirmation, and invoicing are increasingly handled electronically, for example, through EDI or over the Internet. In this way, the administrative tasks as well as the transaction costs of the order cycle are significantly reduced.

Customer service

The term "customer service" includes a number of services before, during, and after the actual sales transaction. Pre-services can, for example, be advising, a flexible and easy ordering process, and easily accessible product information. Service possibilities during the actual order process include a short order cycle, a strong level of warehouse service, and electronically accessible delivery information (track-and-trace, proof-of-delivery). Service after the transaction may encompass various forms of customer support, including installation and assistance in the use of products, maintenance service, guarantees, and return services in the event of error or deficiency.

Distribution
Distribution is specified as the process starting with the completion of the products until their receipt by the customer. In some situations, distribution can also include replacement parts and return transport of damaged, outdated, or scrapped products. Distribution can at times consist of different levels of warehousing, including geographically dependent warehousing. Increasingly, external cooperative partners manage distribution in the so-called TPL (third party logistics) business, which demands great amounts of cooperation and a systematic assessment of the service level as well as logistics costs.

Product development
Previously, product development was an activity carried out in isolation from the daily production. Today, though, product development normally involves close communication with ongoing production. This tendency is demonstrated through such terms as *concurrent engineering*, which involves the initiation of production in coordination with continuing improvements of processes and working procedures. Nonetheless, there is often a key supplier, who is included early on in the product development sequence as a sparring partner during the development of prototypes, and to aid in the choosing of components as well as materials. In addition, customer focus groups are often used to judge and comment on the functionality and market relevance of product ideas. This process ensures that non-viable product ideas are eliminated as soon as possible, increasing the possibility of a high hit rate in the company's product development.

The goal of these activities is to speed up product development, so that time-to-market can be reduced. Time-to-market includes the activities that are connected with the development of new products to be launched on the market. Time-to-market is also a measurement of the speed at which a company is able to transform product ideas into saleable products. This time span is determined by a number of factors, for example: the industry to which the business belongs, the resources the company has at its disposal for R&D, the speed at which technological developments are processed, and the speed at which the needs and preferences of the market change. In the biotech industry, time-to-market can range between 5-10 years, while in the electronic industry, time-to-market is often less than six months. In most industries great emphasis is placed on reducing the time-to-market.

Supply

This process includes all of the activities from choosing a vendor, coming to an agreement on framework contracts, and the continued organising of purchasing. The supply process has changed from being characterised by routine to becoming a strategic process. One of the explanations for this change is the increasing tendency to outsource production processes to the supplier link in the supply chain. Establishing framework agreements/contracts makes it possible to initiate an optimisation of all supply processes, for example, by exchanging information on product plans, warehouse inventories, and sales forecasts, as well as creating procedures for quality control in order to avoid repetitive procedures.

Companies such as B&O, Dell, Nokia, and Oticon are increasingly using vendor-managed inventories (VMI), which presuppose a tight cooperative relationship between customer and supplier, with a continuous exchange of information concerning production plans, stock levels, and sales forecasts.

Management components

SCM's *management components* are a third element in the SCM reference framework. There are a number of management components, which span business processes and the roles of participants in the supply chain. It is of key importance to be aware of these common components in order to secure the successful completion of a supply chain project, because they determine how the individual processes are managed and how they are integrated.

Lambert (1998) divides these components into two main groups:
- Physical and technical components
- Operational and behavioural components

The physical and technical management components can be divided into subcategories:
- Planning and control systems
- Process structure
- Organisational structure
- Information distribution
- Production flow

Planning and control systems are the core of a supply chain. Planning and control include not only activities in the individual company, but also cooperative planning and control of activities and processes throughout the supply chain. Cooperative planning ensures that the supply chain moves in the desired direction, while control ensures that the actual results for the entire supply chain can be compared with the projected goals on an ongoing basis.

Process structure is an indicator of how the company executes its activities and assignments. In this way, a general perspective can form the basis on which common routines for activities within the supply chain can be constructed. The degree of process integration between companies within the supply chain indicates how process oriented the supply chain is.

Organisation structure shows how integrated the different functional departments within the business are, as well as the extent to which integration between the distinct participants in the supply chain takes place. The existence of cross-functional teams within a business and interorganisational teams demonstrates the supply chain's process orientation. This orientation can be exemplified in the transfer of employees for shorter or longer periods to a cooperative partner in the supply chain. Another example could be the existence of cooperative development projects.

The structure of information flow has great influence on the supply chain's effectiveness.

Information exchange between affected departments and companies is decisive if the development and adaptation of cooperative resources and goals are to become possible. Therefore it is relevant to include questions such as: Which types of information are available to the other supply chain participants? How often and in how much detail are the cooperative partners informed? How is information transferred in the supply chain? Are the information systems integrated or real-time based, or is the information typed in each time a legal company boundary is crossed?

The structure of product flow tells something about the complexity of the control activity. Does the product go through a large number of sequential production processes, or is the production structure quite simple? Are there many different suppliers for the components and processes?

Are product development and the commercialisation of new products integrated in the ongoing process? Are suppliers and other relevant cooperative partners involved in the product development process early on?

The operational and behavioural components include:
- Management principles
- Power structure
- Payment/Wage structure
- Company culture

Management principles encompass the company's philosophy and the management methods and philosophies that dominate the businesses in focus. If, for example, the overall management principles support a strong hierarchical decision-making process, with solid routines and a clear definition of responsibility and specialisation, it is difficult to alter these principles to a more flexible, cross-organisational cooperative structure.

The power structure in a supply chain conveys something about who has the potential to affect the participants in a given direction. In practice, there will often be a dominant company within a supply chain, which will take the initiative to implement the SCM concept. The dominant company can use their position of power to impose the desired changes upon their cooperative partners. However, the business can also choose constructive cooperation, where all involved parties can share in the benefits of the SCM concept. The implementation of the SCM concept leads to the creation of a basis for establishing a form of cooperation that makes it possible for all motivated participants to exchange their experience and knowledge, despite the fact that the dominant company controls the goals and initiatives.

The Payment/Wage structure should support the process orientation and not work against it. Function-oriented companies often have budgets and result targets that focus on the efficiency of individual departments and reward the departments and individuals who reach these result targets. If employees need to be motivated across organisational boundaries, then performance goals, which concentrate on the processes instead of the functions, must be established. The reward structure in the supply chain must also reflect the amount of resources at stake for the individual participant, as well as the risks the participant runs by becoming actively involved in SCM cooperation. The reward/bonus for a vendor can, for example, be a long-term contract, a larger portion of the purchasing budget, or competency development. For a customer, examples of a possible reward/bonus could include better customer service, vendor managed inventory, faster response time, cooperative development projects, and/or lower total costs.

Company culture and employee attitudes are important components in SCM cooperation. If the participants in a supply chain come from very different company cultures or if employee attitudes do not complement cooperation, then it is difficult to implement SCM cooperation. Changing a company's culture is a difficult task and in the best-case scenario, takes a long time. Motivating employees to engage in cross-organisational cooperation demands a goal-oriented effort in the form of attitude workshops and continuing-education programmes. Both activities demand persistent efforts on the part of top-management.

Main Types of Supply Chains

The term "supply chain" gives rise to associations of serial cooperation, where materials and products are closely correlated throughout a chain of value-creating activities, which are like pearls on a string. Practically speaking, the relationships between the implicated companies are often quite complex. Some relations can be rather close and stable, while others are more short-term and ad hoc in nature.

The supply network is a more complete term than supply chain. However, "supply chain" is used throughout this book, as Supply Chain Management has become a generally accepted term in the business community.

There are many different types of supply chains. Harland (2001) has suggested four main types, each of which has distinctive characteristics and specific demands on the cooperation between participants. These classifications are based on two dimensions:

- Dynamic versus stable supply chains
- Dominant company versus balanced power distribution in the supply chain

By combining these two dimensions, four generic supply chain types result. These types are shown in Figure 2.2.

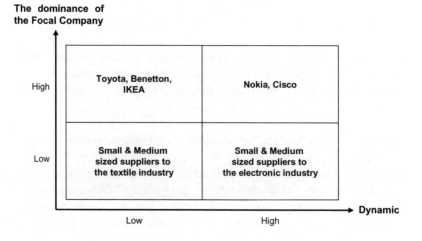

Figure 2.2 shows a 2x2 matrix. The vertical axis is labeled "The dominance of the Focal Company" with "High" and "Low" levels. The horizontal axis is labeled "Dynamic" with "Low" and "High" levels.

- High / Low: Toyota, Benetton, IKEA
- High / High: Nokia, Cisco
- Low / Low: Small & Medium sized suppliers to the textile industry
- Low / High: Small & Medium sized suppliers to the electronic industry

Figure 2.2 Typology of Supply Chains

Type 1: Dynamic/low level of influence from the company in focus

This type operates under dynamic conditions while the company in focus has only limited influence on the other participants involved in the supply chain. The dynamic conditions could be explained by frequent internal process changes, due to multiple product configurations or external market conditions, with a myriad of competitors as well as many new product launches. The low degree of influence exerted by the company in focus may be explained by the fact that the company does not contribute a great degree of value, for example, in the form of volume or innovative products/processes, to the other supply chain participants. In this situation, the most important activities in relation to the other companies involved to motivate them to participate in an integrated cooperation and to secure a fair distribution of risks and benefits. Examples can be found within the smaller sub-vendors in an industry.

Type 2: Dynamic/high degree of influence held by the company in focus

In this type of supply chain the focus company has power/influence over the other participants. In this situation, the focus company will typically, as a result of their purchasing power or innovative ability/image, be an important cooperative partner for the other links in the supply chain. A company such as B&O will, following this principle, be an attractive customer for many suppliers, as it would generally be seen as a mark of quality to be a key supplier to B&O. Another example is Nokia, who, due to their size and innovative product development, will lend value to the images of their customers and suppliers. In this type of example, the focus company will be in a position to pick and choose their cooperative partners rather than being chosen, for example, because they have implemented VMI or because they live up to specific requirements made on retail shops regarding product availability, shop decoration/furnishings, and education of personnel.

Type 3: Static/focus company has a low level of influence

This supply chain works under stable conditions, both internally and externally. Total cost effectiveness will often be the primary aspect of competition. Focus will be on increasing effectiveness within the logistics processes, including improving processes, integrating information systems, reducing inventory, and making full use of capacity. In order to realise these forms of increasing effectiveness, the focus company must be able to motivate the other participants as well as give them a fair portion of the resulting savings relative to the risks that they have taken. Examples can be found among small suppliers in the process industry or the textile industry.

Type 4: Static/focus company has high degree of influence

In this type of supply chain the focus company enjoys a high degree of influence over the other parties involved. This situation indicates that the dominant company can choose its cooperation partners and make the necessary decisions regarding the organisation of the supply chain, as well as increasing its effectiveness. A typical focus company of this type would be IKEA, whose product line can remain stable over a long period of time.

This illustrated classification of the main types of supply chains can aid the individual company in its effort to identify the type it most closely resembles, and which activities the company should focus on when building relationships with other companies.

What is Supply Chain Integration?

Bowersox, Closs and Stank (2002) have classified integration in a supply chain context into six different types: customer integration, internal integration, material and service supplier integration, technology and planning integration, measurement integration, and relationship integration.

Stevens (1989) identifies four stages of supply chain integration, where Stage I represents the fragmented operations within the individual company. Stage II focuses on limited integration between adjacent functions, e.g. purchasing and materials control. Stage III requires the internal integration of the end-to-end planning in the individual company and Stage IV represents true supply chain integration, both upstream to suppliers and downstream to customers.

Lee (2000) outlines three dimensions of supply chain integration: information integration, coordination and resource sharing, and organisational relationship linkages. Information integration refers to the sharing of information and knowledge among the members in the supply chain, including sales forecasts, production plans, inventory status and promotion plans. Coordination and resource sharing refers to the realignment of decisions and responsibility in the supply chain. Organisational relationship linkages include communication channels between the members in the supply chain, performance measurement and sharing of common visions and objectives.

Information Technology

In this book, focus is on the information related to the flows of materials, products and services, including the reverse flows contained in a logistics information system (LIS). Information integration permits management to examine the operations of the organisation as a whole and not in a fragmented, functionally isolated manner. Similarly, the participants in a supply chain can be linked by information technology, thereby facilitating such logistics activities as inventory management, order fulfilment, production planning, and delivery planning and coordination. Business needs drive managers to become more competitive and they are under increased pressure to integrate the supply chain.

Integration often requires coordination of disparate functions among supply chain partners in geographically dispersed locations. Information integration also involves the sharing of pertinent knowledge and information among members of a supply chain. It may involve the sharing of design and manufacturing data among suppliers, focal manufacturers, and customers. It may also include sharing forecast and delivery scheduling data between the logistics functions of the customers, the focal company, the suppliers, the carriers, and the other members of the supply chain.

Suppliers and customers may be invited to participate in focal company product design teams to capture pertinent upstream and downstream issues in the product/process designs to reduce costly design and/or process changes later. Information integration makes inventory and production visible throughout the supply chain, creating a more congenial climate for collaborative planning and forecasting. Supply chain members, as a result, face less uncertainty, can reduce inventory buffers by postponing costly value-adding operations and provide better customer service, including more flexible responses to customer demand.

A reliable communication infrastructure paves the way for timely and efficient information exchange among partners. For example, using electronic data interchange (EDI) technology, manufacturers can provide up-to-the-minute information about their production needs by giving vendors access to the production planning and control system and vendors can arrange deliveries without the need of any paper transactions.

Similarly, timely payments can be arranged using EDI. Reduction of payment delays lowers the cost of doing business significantly, makes supply chains more efficient, and gives the users a competitive advantage. The integration of the many IT-enabled electronic commerce tools – bar coding, electronic messaging, electronic data interchange, global network management, and the Internet – allows supply chain partners to attain significant productivity gains. The fruits of information integration, such as reduced cycle time from order to delivery, increased visibility of transactions, better tracing and tracking, reduced transaction costs, and enhanced customer service offer greater competitive advantage for all participants in the supply chain.

Organisational Integration
Organisational integration encourages partners to become more entrenched members of the network and instils a sense of belonging to the supply chain. It becomes easier to generate trust among partners in an integrated supply chain. Trust promotes collaboration and decision delegation, and reduces irrational behaviour and "second guessing" among supply chain members, thereby reducing the need for safety stocks. The objective of organisational integration is not merely to

resolve conflicts should they arise, but rather to recognise and avoid potential conflicts and/or divergences of interest in advance and devise a governance structure to forestall or avoid them. True organisational integration thus paves the way for individual members of the chain to behave more like a single unified entity sharing ideas, skills and culture alike. Supply chain integration may fail to blossom without organisational integration among supply chain partners.

Supply chain management may require various actors at all levels of hierarchy in multiple organisations to work together to achieve a common goal. Managing coordination among the supply chain partners therefore assumes significant importance. Organisational integration can become a catalyst by facilitating information sharing within and among firms. Some researchers opine that flat organisations work better than cumbersome hierarchical ones. Some have suggested that process-oriented organisational structures will work better than traditional hierarchical structures in networks with many partners.

Another organisational issue is the realignment of activities in a supply chain. Where should the activities and processes be located across the collaborating firms? Who should take responsibility for decisions? Under what conditions should a particular activity be outsourced? The transaction cost approach (Williamson, 1996) gives some normative prescriptions for this issue. The transaction cost approach recommends that in situations with transaction-specific investments, the activities should be performed within the hierarchy that is vertically integrated within the firm. In situations with low asset specificity, the transactions should be performed in the marketplace. Finally, in situations with medium asset specificity, a hybrid organisation structure is the most suitable. In most supply chain collaborations between organisations, we expect to find manifestations of medium asset specificity as defined by Williamson. These assets can be either physical or knowledge based. In situations of medium asset specificity, these assets are not entirely dedicated to the specific relationship between the partners. These can be redirected to alternative uses should the partnership fail to materialise or break.

Innovative or Functional Products?

Fisher (1997) found that if one classifies products on the basis of their demand patterns, they fall into one of two categories: primarily innovative or primarily functional. Each category requires a distinctly different kind of supply chain integration. This is illustrated in table 2.1.

	Physically Efficient Process	**Market-Responsive Process**
Primary purpose	supply predictable demand efficiently at the lowest possible cost	Respond quickly to unpredictable demand in order to minimize stockouts, forced markdowns, and obsolete inventory
Manufacturing focus	maintain high average utilization rate	Deploy excess buffer capacity
Inventory strategy	generate high turns and minimize inventory throughout the chain	Deploy significant buffer of parts or finished goods
Lead-time focus	shorten lead time as long as it doesn't increase cost	Invest aggressively in ways to reduce lead time
Approach to choosing suppliers	select primarily for cost and quality	Select primarily for speed, flexibility, and quality
Product-design strategy	maximize performance and minimize cost	Use modular design in order to postpone product differentiation for as long as possible

Table 2.1 Efficient and responsive supply chains

Firms that compete with innovative products and technology have less incentive to share sensitive product and/or business information with supply chain partners. Therefore, we would expect them to have a relatively low degree of integration with their supply chain partners. That is not to say that these firms do not enter into partnerships in supply chains, but they often restrict this activity to the sharing of information in order to ensure a smooth flow of materials. However, when it comes to core competence areas, they are not very interested in sharing information with supply chain members. While there may be very close partnerships between these firms culminating in sharing planning and logistics data, partners are not likely to join forces on the design and development of core items.

Volvo[2] works in close partnership with 15 key suppliers located in a supplier park close to Volvo's assembly plant. These key suppliers share procurement and delivery data on a real time basis. They are given various forms of assistance to ensure the high quality and timeliness of their supplies. Often they are invited to technology and management forums organised by Volvo and future production plans are shared with key suppliers up to a year in advance in order to offer them adequate lead time to organise production changes. However, when it comes to core items such as engines or body platforms, the suppliers are joint ventures or subsidiaries of Volvo. Only a few suppliers are invited to participate in core design teams and the company does not trust external entities to supply technology or systems in core areas such as engine, transmission or safety engineering, elements that give Volvo distinctive competences in the marketplace.

For companies offering primarily functional products with a fairly stable and predictable demand and long life cycles, the incentive to integrate with their supply chain partners is high as these products naturally attract more competition, thereby enhancing the need for cost efficiency. Here, we would expect extensive use of collaborative planning and design, continuous improvements, vendor managed inventory (VMI), continuous replenishment programmes (CRP), dedicated account teams and frequent exchange of personnel. An example is Wal-Mart's collaboration with Pfizer on the forecasting and replenishment of over-the-counter pharmaceuticals and healthcare products. Wal-Mart has more knowledge of the customers' preferences, while Pfizer knows about the drugs it produces and is better equipped to make use of external data, such as weather forecasts and pollen figures, to estimate demand patterns.

When it comes to more functional products, manufacturers often invite key suppliers to participate in the design process in order to accelerate time to market. An example is Dell Computers, which works closely with its key suppliers when it comes to designing common platforms across several products and using common components. Dell's competitive strategy is the capability of designing products that are easy to customise. By sharing design databases and methodologies with key suppliers, Dell Computers is able to increase the speed of time to market - often dramatically.

---

[2] Based on Bagchi & Skjoett-Larsen (2002)

Governance Structure

Using similar reasoning, it is easy to see why a firm marketing a new product in the early phase of its life cycle would not be keen to engage in a close inter-organisational relationship with its supply chain partners. This view also receives support from the transaction cost approach. The basic premise of transaction cost theory is that governance is the mechanism through which a firm manages an economic exchange. For standard off-the-shelf types of items or functional products, firms rely on *market governance* when they interact with other firms. For innovative products and during the early stages of product life cycle, firms usually rely more on product-specific assets, for example, specialized knowledge and process skills or technology, owned by them. In other words, at the early stages of a product's life cycle, firms use *hierarchical governance* where the required assets are available within the boundaries of the firm. At a mature stage of a product's life cycle, when more competitors have entered the market and competition has been intensified, firms may try to leverage supply chain partners' complementary skills in addition to their own in order achieve higher cost efficiency and stay competitive. This push to become more competitive leads to what is called *intermediate governance* in transaction cost theory when alliances with supply chain partners are resorted to and inter-organisational integration results.

The Italian clothing company Benetton was for many years the archetype of the network organisation, that is, an organisation based on outsourcing, subcontracting and developing relationships in a tiered structure of supplier networks. Benetton used to outsource the labour-intensive phases of production, such as tailoring, finishing and ironing, to small and medium-sized companies. However, the relatively more innovative operations, such as design, quality control and dyeing, or operations that required heavy investment (weaving, cutting, pick-pack and storage) have always been performed in-house. Benetton has recently moved to more upscale clothing and transformed its global network (Camuffo, 2001). Upstream, they have gradually increased vertical integration of textile and thread suppliers to ensure direct control over the supply of materials and exercise quality control sooner. Benetton can then send the materials directly to the production facilities without further checks and thereby reduce both transport costs and production lead times. Downstream, they have set up a number of mega stores throughout the world owned and managed by

Benetton itself. This allows Benetton to get closer to end customers and collect data on their last-minute needs and expectations. At the same time, Benetton has reduced the basic product assortment and increased the number of flash seasonal collections to respond faster to changes in market trends. In other words, as Benetton transforms its product line from relatively more functional products to relatively more fashionable clothing, it is restructuring its organisation from an intermediate governance structure consisting of supply chain integration to a more hierarchical governance mechanism resorting to vertical integration.

Industry Maturity

An industry in the early phase of its life cycle exhibits a high degree of uncertainty and changing technology. While products may certainly be more innovative in nature, their design and technology keeps evolving. The industry is often in a state of flux. Above all, during this phase, firms and organisations also tend to safeguard their selfish interests of acquiring as much market share as possible. Companies in such situations tend to discourage too close partnerships with external entities and are generally averse to sharing too much sensitive information for very obvious reasons.

At the early phases of a product's life cycle, companies are busy trying to cash in on their proprietary technology in order to secure a competitive position in the market. Accordingly, firms try to organise all activities such as manufacturing, sales and marketing, logistics, distribution and service support within the firm boundaries. As customers, dealers and other service providers become more knowledgeable of the technology and as the reliability of the products improves (so that service requirements decrease), the manufacturers do not feel the same compulsion to maintain total control of all activities. The success of IBM in relation to Sperry-Rand is often traced to the intensive service support that IBM provided for its then relatively unfamiliar but complex product in the 1950s. Today, external vendors contracted by the manufacturers often provide after-sales service support.

Also, as industries mature and firms dig in and consolidate market share, the scale of production is increased, uncertainty is reduced and products and processes undergo standardisation. In a less uncertain environment, companies experience less need for vertical integration. Additionally, as the scale of production increases, asset specificity increases as general-purpose flexible machinery makes room for automated and dedicated capital equipment for achieving higher operational efficiency. The scale of investment required rises proportionately, putting it beyond the reach of most firms and thus creating a natural barrier to entry. Therefore, in a mature industry, while there is more intense competition, it is frequently the case that there is no single company that produces everything. Instead, companies become more open to close inter-organisational relationships with capable external entities for the efficient provision of products and services. It is easy to argue that as firms find investment needs beyond their reach, they adopt more pragmatic strategies and look for supply chain partners who can complement their capabilities and resources. Thus, as products and processes mature and undergo standardisation, companies begin to rely more heavily on the market for recurrent acquisition of parts and components, which leads to greater supply chain integration.

The emerging contract production industry further illustrates this trend. Contract firms have built up competences within a well-defined part of the total production process. By offering production capabilities to global OEM companies, they can achieve high efficiency and speed in their operations as well as economies of scale. Contract production is growing within the areas of fashion goods, electronics and chemical and pharmaceutical processes. For example, Flextronics and Solectron have taken over the assembly of mobile phones for Ericsson, Nokia and Siemens.

Dominance and Supply Chain Integration

Power is seldom distributed equally among participants in a supply chain. A firm's power in a supply chain represents its potential for influence on other participants' attitudes and behaviour. Often, one participant has a dominant position, either because of purchasing power, market share, or access to proprietary technology and knowledge. In the automotive industry, car manufacturers are often in a dominant position relative to the suppliers and can influence the upstream supply chain. In the grocery industry, the large retailers are the dominant players and can dictate the conditions for collaboration even with the major brand manufacturers such as P&G, Unilever and Nestlé.

LEGO Company (net sales in 2003 1,1 billion Euro and 8.200 employees), the Danish manufacturer of construction toys, makes a large percentage of its total sales through five retail chains in the US.

LEGO Company is interested in developing strong relationships with their key customers. However, large customers such as Toys-"R"-Us, Wal-Mart and K-Mart wield the real power to initiate collaboration in the supply chain. LEGO Company receives point-of-sale data from their large customers and also participates in automatic replenishment programmes. However, LEGO Company is decoupled from direct access to end customers and their expectations and preferences.
www.LEGO.com

Power or dominance is therefore an important factor in determining the extent to which a supply chain is suitable for integration and the level of supply chain integration. In supply chains where one firm is highly dependent on the other participants but not vice versa, the less dependent firms will have a power advantage and can force strong and effective relationships in the supply chain. In situations where there is a low degree of dependency between the dominant firm and the other firms in the supply chain, one would expect to find low integration. Supply chain integration blossoms when the self-seeking dominant partner is convinced of the need for integration and takes the initiative to mobilise all partners.

In the case of a supply chain that enjoys a high degree of dominance in a market with low competition, low integration is to be expected.

Carlsberg Brewery, which has a market share of about 80% in the Danish market, is an interesting example. By virtue of its dominant position in the Danish market, Carlsberg decides the level and extent of supply chain integration it desires. With little or no competition around, the company is happy to hang on to its market share and experiences no significant pressure to improve. The opposite is true in the UK market, where there is heavy competition between the different market players and where access to consumers is vital for survival. Here, vertical integration, joint ventures or strategic alliances are common in order to get access to or control over the distribution channels, including the pubs.
www.carlsberg.com[3]

If on the contrary the dominant player is operating in a competitive environment, the company can be expected to be more proactive, and

---

[3] Read more about Carlsberg in Chapter 5.

aim for high integration with their supply chain partners. Examples can be found in the automotive industry and the fashion industry.

However, if none of the partners in a supply chain has a dominant position and the market competition is relatively low, a stable situation with a low degree of integration is likely to arise. The building construction industry could serve as an example of this. In highly competitive market situations and balanced power relationships among the participants in the supply chain, the degree of integration depends very much on the industry culture and traditions. In some industries, limited integration and a reactive adoption of new technology are likely to occur. In other industries, there might be a tradition for collaboration and specialisation. For instance, in industrial districts in northern Italy small firms collaborate very closely in networks and with highly sophisticated technology. Examples are found within fashion clothes, ceramic tiles, and leather and shoe industries.

Different Levels of SCM Cooperation

SCM in its pure form cannot be found in any supply chain. SCM should be thought of as a vision towards, which a company can work. There are many stages in the realisation of the grand SCM solution, and it can be advantageous to progress through these stages step by step, even though one may chose to stop at some point along the way. The implementation of the SCM concept will always be contingent on the specific situation. That is, a number of specific factors will be decisive in terms of how far the concrete working relationship progresses towards integrated coordination. Figure 2.3 illustrates different levels of SCM cooperation. The x-axis shows the level of integration while the y-axis measures the degree of complexity.

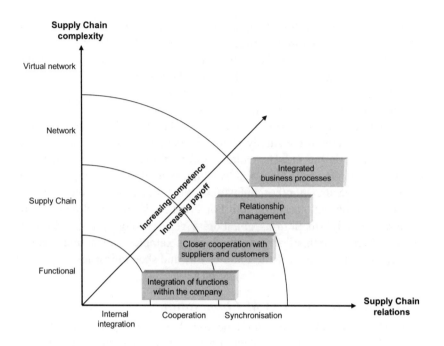

Figure 2.3 Integration levels in SCM cooperation

The level of integration demonstrates how closely coordination and cooperation are synchronised among the relevant parties. These levels can, for example, be measured by the openness for, and possibility of exchanging information online between the supply chain participants. Other examples include cross-organisational teams, exchanging employees, the number of contact points between the companies, and shared product development.

The degree of information exchange can be demonstrated by the openness the involved parties show towards each other in regard to sharing cost calculations, production plans, sales forecasts, development of new products and markets, and implementation of new technology. Figure 2.3 indicates that the closer one comes to the right corner, the greater the requirements become for the participants' competence levels, as well as their ability to handle complicated relationships.

Level 1 includes integration and cooperation within the area of the supply chain that the individual company controls. This integration can be exemplified in an ERP system, which allows all decision makers' access to a shared database. Coordination between the different areas can be promoted by establishing representative teams, and by holding regular meetings between representatives of the different departments/areas.

Level 2 takes the process one step further and establishes more long-term cooperation with strategically important customers, suppliers, or logistics companies. This cooperation will often involve the out-sourcing to cooperative partners of activities that had previously been internal. In order to cooperate on this level, partners must know each other thoroughly through prior business transactions. Additional key attributes for this level of cooperation include a degree of confidence in the cooperative partners' competences and a certain amount of openness to the sharing of information, for example, each others' calculations, also referred to as "open-book". Some form of common goals is also typical of this level.

Level 3 expands the cooperation to include activities close to the companies' core competences. For example, the dominant company in a supply chain may involve strategic vendors in the product development process in order to ensure that the suppliers' qualifications match the requirements of the future cooperation. The goal of these actions can also be the utilisation of knowledge possessed by key suppliers concerning process technology and material characteristics. Finally, an early-stage integration of vendors can also reduce the time span between the idea phase and the marketing of a new product. At this level, cooperation is supported by cooperation contracts, which often include a number of target points, also referred to as critical success factors.

Level 4 represents the highest level of integration between companies in a supply chain. Strong demands on partners to have a high degree of openness with regard to exchanging information, mutually binding investments, and ability to cooperate, are key characteristics of this level. Cross-company integration of business processes can dominate and the boundaries between companies become looser in level 4. Employees are not bound to a specific position in a specific company, but can be placed at a cooperating company for periods of time. The companies' information systems are integrated and all relevant information for planning and process controlling is available in real time to the supply chain participants. Product development is initiated on the basis of strong cooperation between the customer, the manufacturer, and the supplier. Cooperation is delineated in a cooperation contract, including a shared set of target goals. Cooperative partners' top managers are actively involved in the integration process.

The descriptions of the four levels of integration between companies in a supply chain presented above are naturally simplifications. In practice, there are many forms of integration, which blend elements from the different levels. A development process for the implementation of the SCM concept from one level to another is not necessarily represented in these four levels, even though most companies move through different phases before SCM cooperation is realised. The goal is not to make all relationships to vendors and customers fit the description of level 4. The point is to develop and care for these relationships, so that the "best fit" can be achieved. In other words, the benefits companies can offer each other should be utilised, but time should not be wasted on projects, services, and activities that do not generate increased value for the supply chain. This point is illustrated in Figure 2.4.

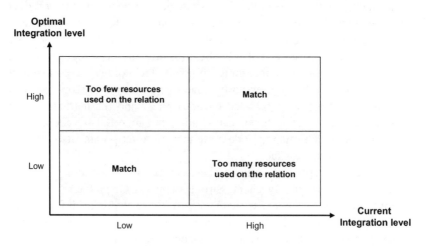

Figure 2.4 Portfolio analysis of relations

The company should analyse its business-related relations and prioritise its efforts in accordance with the strategic implications each relationship represents. Practically speaking, the applied resources are often conversely related to the importance of the relationship. It is not uncommon that the company uses more resources on a difficult customer, who only comprises a minor portion of the company's business, while few resources are applied to developing cooperative relationships with strategic customers who "don't make noise."

Table 2.2 outlines a classification of the different degrees of "maturity" within SCM. Maturity can be measured in many ways. The classification illustrated is by its very nature subjective. Despite these qualifiers, the two extremes can be used in benchmarking for companies that wish to judge how far they have come in their SCM cooperation, as well as how they can continue to progress in the process.

	Early stages of SCM	Advanced stages of SCM
Information Systems	• MRP II systems in production planning • No EDI links to external cooperation partners • Low/poor degree of system integration • Barcoding only on final products • Internet/Extranet used primarily for correspondence	• ERP system implemented • APS systems used as decision support • EDI links to important cooperation partners • Use of barcodes to track-and-trace throughout the supply chain • ECR with important customers • Internet/Extranet used in purchasing and sales • VMI with selected customers • CRM/SRM for management of customer/vendor base
Organisation Form	• Primarily functional oriented • Logistics/SCM not represented at the level of the director • Fragmented logistics function • SCM not a part of the company's business model • Few points of contact between the companies in the supply chain	• Primarily process oriented • Logistics/SCM represented at the director level • Teams, both across functional borders and between companies • SCM is an important component in the company's business model • Many contact points between companies • Focus on management of relations regarding the use of SRM and CRM.

Information Exchange	• Ordering by fax, phone., or e-mail • Access to customer/supplier warehouse status • Harmonising of warehouse stocks in the supply chain	• Ordering by Internet/extranet • Production planes and sales prognoses accessible for suppliers • Vendors included in product development • Mutual access to cost calculations
Time dimension	• Contracts of limited duration • Regular bidding rounds to test the market	• Contracts with longer timelines and agreed-upon efficiency goals • Continuous benchmarking in order to secure high efficiency and quality • Contract renegotiation without market testing
Measuring and Management	• Measuring of delivery service • Measuring of the degree of warehouse service • Measuring of logistics costs	• Performance goals on all business processes • Continuous vendor evaluation • Measurement of customer service

Table 2.2 Stages of "maturity" in implementation of SCM

What Characterises Successful SCM Cooperation?

Experiences from implementing the SCM concept in European companies show that the following attributes typically characterise successful SCM cooperation:

• Strategic SCM implementation. The first item of clarification must be how SCM can be incorporated in the overall business strategy. This stage also includes making clear, which resources shall be allocated, who will be involved in the SCM cooperation etc. The implementation of the SCM concept internally and in relation to cooperation partners is a process that affects activities in many areas. These areas include purchasing, production, planning, and sales. It is therefore crucial that the top-level managers follow the process with interest and are active and prepared to maintain the direction, and are also capable of executing the necessary decisions.

- Frequent and reciprocal information exchange between actors regarding inventory status, forecasts, production plans, sales and marketing strategies etc. The goal is to reduce uncertainty and reaction time for the entire supply chain. Ideally, the information is as readily accessible to all parties as it is for any single participant in the SCM cooperation. Here the emphasis is on ensuring transparency in the supply chain so that the individual participant can plan activities based on information that is as reliable as possible.

- "Fair" sharing of the advantages and risks with SCM cooperation, making the individual participant feel that the rewards of entering into the cooperative effort are evenly balanced between the resources invested and the risk of loss. Otherwise, the incentive to continue cooperating disappears. In the beginning of a SCM project there is a harmonisation of the expectations and goals between the actors in the supply chain. The resource contribution will often be unevenly divided among the cooperating partners. Therefore, it is important with regard to long-term cooperation that participants, who invest a relatively large amount of resources receive a corresponding proportion of the rationalisation gains. This equitable distribution can help ensure long-term contracts, joint investments in production equipment, and agreements as to the sharing of cost savings.

- Development of integrated information systems among actors. Today, many companies have implemented ERP systems (Enterprise Resource Planning) such as SAP, PeopleSoft, Oracle, BAAN, Movex, and Navision. These systems make it possible to integrate activities and processes within the individual company, and offer the potential to transfer information to other actors via EDI/Internet/Intranet. ERP systems are, for the time being, primarily transaction systems, which both register transactions and make them accessible to all relevant decision makers through a joint database system. In recent years the so-called APS systems (Advanced Planning and Scheduling) have been developed. These systems give management a tool to make better decisions for the whole supply chain. The best-known software programmes are Manugistics, i2 Technologies, Axapta, and SAP APO.

- Openness and trust between cooperation partners. Trust can only develop over time. As a result, the cooperating parties must have the possibility of working together for a longer period of time. Trust can be demonstrated by informing each other about development plans, visions and strategies, and by allowing open access to calculations, by using "single sourcing," and by sharing ideas on, for example, product development, where relevant for cooperation.

- Credible commitments between the involved parties. Commitments can be demonstrated through, for example, long-term contracts, investments in customer-specific assets, employee exchange, and joint competency development.

- Organisational adaptation and proportional risk adjustment among all involved parties. These characteristics could, for example be demonstrated through inter-organisational teams, projects with representatives from the involved companies, or mutual exchange of key employees, designed to increase knowledge of each other's companies. The goal is to create a process-oriented attitude among employees, while focusing on the entire supply chain. Most companies are organised around the principle of functionality, which can give rise to complications in connection with SCM cooperation. Employees filling the roles that will be integrated in a SCM project need to develop an understanding of how to participate interactively in the activities of the total supply chain.

- The use of customers' needs and desires as a starting point. Performance targets for a company in the supply chain should result from focusing on customer satisfaction and customer loyalty. Order-to -delivery time, flexibility, and efficiency are measured in relation to the final customer, not through comparison to intermediaries in the supply chain. However, it is also important to establish intermediate goals, which can increase the visibility of the contribution made by each link to the total goal.

Table 2.3 summarises the most important characteristics of a traditional "arm's length" approach and an SCM approach.

Element	Traditional cooperation	SCM cooperation
Inventory control	Independent inventory reduction	Coordinated and total inventory reduction throughout the supply chain
Cost focus	Minimising companies' logistical costs	Minimising the supply chain's total costs
Time horizon	Short term	Long term
Information sharing	Limited to current transactions	All information relevant for planning and control of the integrated processes in the supply chain
Supplier base	Many suppliers, multi-sourcing	Reduction of vendor base, single or dual sourcing, also prioritising of relationship level
Organisational type	Functional organisation	Process oriented
Sharing of risks and gains	Each actor seeks to optimise own risks and gains	Fair sharing of risks and gains, proportional to contribution
Information systems	Not integrated	Integrated and compatible Edi/Internet
Goals and vision	Not harmonised between companies	Shared idea of goals and vision
Focus	Succeeding downstream intermediary	End customer
Contract type	Classic contract	Relational contract/partnership

Table 2.3 A Comparison of Traditional Cooperation and SCM Cooperation

B&O – an Example of Supplier Segmentation

Bang & Olufsen (B&O)[4] is an internationally renowned producer of audio-visual equipment characterised by high quality, advanced design, and consistent functionality. In 2003/04 B&O had a turnover of approximately 500 million Euro, 85% of which was export. B&O has about 2,300 employees. Sales are handled by a number of independent

---

[4] The case is based upon personal interviews with staff members of B&O Operations.

agents and 12 national sales companies, which are 100% owned by B&O. There are roughly 2,100 dealers in 40 countries.

In 2000, a restructuring took place under the name Bang & Olufsen United. B&O was divided into an stock-exchange listed company, Bang & Olufsen A/S, and a number of corporations, which were 100% owned by B&O. B&O AudioVisual is the largest company and is responsible for development and sales of B&O's audio-visual products, with focus on global distribution development. B&O Telecom develops and markets new telephone concepts. B&O New Business develops new business areas, with B&O's competences and market position as its starting point. An example is ICEpower, based on highly effective speaker technology, of which B&O owns 75% of the share capital. B&O Operations manages purchasing, production, and logistics for the group. Finally, B&O Medicon, which applies B&O's competences to the medical field, produces, for example, insulin pens for Novo Nordisk.

B&O's Supply Chain

During the last decade, B&O's supply chain has undergone a number of dramatic changes. In the mid 80's B&O experienced an economic crisis with a red bottom line. B&O had to sell 25% of its share capital to the Philips group in order to survive. Under a new Managing Director, a number of production, logistics, sales, and product development initiatives were carried out, the so-called break-point project.

One of these initiatives was a large logistics project, which had as its goal to increase B&O's earnings by:

• Improving the customer service level
• Reducing inventory capital binding

The logistics project was communicated internally through a number of seminars and courses, in which a large number of employees participated. Additionally, a small handbook, "Logistics at Bang & Olufsen – The customer in the centre" was given to all employees. The handbook explained the term logistics and B&O's goal for logistics in an readily understandable way. The goals for the logistics concept were as follows:

• Vendors should be able to alter deliveries by 30% within maximum 40 working days.

- All intermediate processes before final assembly should be completely within a maximum of 10 working days.
- Finally assembly for all orders should occur within two working days.
- Delivery time from the time the customer orders to delivery to the dealer may not exceed five working days.

Figure 2.5 shows B&O's supply chain

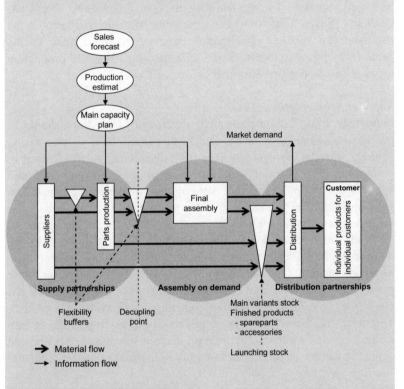

Figure 2.5 B&O's Supply Chain

B&O has worked systematically towards these goals. The production side has been addressed by outsourcing a number of non-core activities to vendors and by establishing a differentiated supply strategy. Production itself has been restructured into electronic production, mechanical production, and final assembly. Distribution has been centralised, the subsidiaries' inventories have been eliminated, and distribution goes directly to a dealer or the final customer. At the same time, distribution has been outsourced to a few third party logistics companies. The dealer network has been more strongly profiled with focus on concept stores, the so-called B1 retailer. In 2004 B&O has established approximately 650 B1 shops, which account for about 70% of the total revenue.

From the beginning of the 90's B&O's logistics concept was based on a strategy of speculation, both in production and distribution. Most products were produced in batches and placed in inventory. From that point, they were distributed to sales companies in Europe, which managed inventory for the national markets. Since 1990, B&O has gradually moved away from the speculation strategy and towards the postponement strategy. Inventories have been pulled back to the central warehouse in Denmark and an increasing amount of production today is based on actual customer orders.

Supplier Segmentation Model

Previously, B&O had the philosophy that roughly everything should be produced in-house. In 1993 B&O introduced a new purchasing strategy whereby new trends were more dynamically incorporated in purchasing. The supplier base was reduced from 1000 to 300, and components and processes that were not part of the core competences were outsourced. The total purchasing volume today is more than 300 million Euro, and suppliers account for 85-90% of the costs of materials and 50% of the development costs. Most standard tasks are outsourced to subcontractors, including moulding of large plastic elements, bending and punching projects, as well as all iron and wire production. Recently, the electronic factory was outsourced to the electronic manufacturing service company Flextronics International. The mechanic factory focuses on advanced plastic moulding, as well as ceramic and mechanic aluminium surface treatments. Finally, the assembly factory handles final assembly of customer specific products.

B&O's purchasing department has undergone three stages of development since 1993:
1. Partner relations, including reduction of the vendor base and outsourcing of production (1993-98).
2. Systems relations, encompassing several assembly-ready components and fewer intermediate components (1998-2001).
3. Business relations – composed of a business-oriented cost efficiency project as well as a differentiated supplier strategy (2002-2005).

In 2000, B&O developed a new sourcing strategy, which includes a number of goals for pricing, logistics, quality, and technology. The goals for logistics are:
- An average lead time of three weeks
- A delivery precision of 98%
- Electronic purchasing
- An inventory turnover rate of 13 times a year

In connection with the sourcing strategy, a model for supplier segmentation has been developed. This model is shown in Figure 2.6.

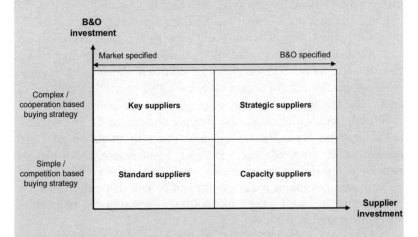

Figure 2.6 B&O's Segmenting Model for Suppliers

As shown in the figure, B&O distinguishes between four types of suppliers:
- Standard Suppliers
- Capacity Suppliers
- Key suppliers
- Strategic suppliers

Standard Suppliers
Suppliers of standard products or "commodities" typically find themselves in a quite competitive market, where price and delivery terms are determining factors. There is always an alternative source, which can offer the same general price and quality. Continuous assessments of the market are made based on price, logistics, and quality. If a more optimal supplier is located, then initiatives are taken

to ensure that they are used. Relationships between buyer and vendor are characterised by an "arm's length" attitude. In the future, this type of purchasing will occur electronically, enabling the buyer to compare price, quality, and services between different suppliers. B&O aims to reduce the number of suppliers within this segment.

Capacity Suppliers

Capacity suppliers are vendors that execute relatively simple production tasks according to specifications developed by B&O. An example of this type of service could include simple assembly assignments, limited process tasks such as drilling holes, as well as the sanding and bending of metal pieces. Capacity suppliers are typically used for limited periods when B&O experiences peak loads in their own production. Supplier relations are differentiated depending on the task and supplier. The aim is to establish "open and honest" relationships, so that the vendor knows whether or not they are "in" or "out." The market is thoroughly researched for new potential suppliers in order to secure alternative sourcing possibilities at the international level. Suppliers are evaluated regularly, primarily based on price and quality. It is expected that vendors can consistently demonstrate improvements in their efficiency and productivity. If repeated performance deviations occur on the part of one particular vendor, a new vendor is found. B&O focuses on minimising the number of suppliers in this category.

Key Suppliers

Key suppliers are suppliers that possess key technologies that are critical for the customer company's final product. By purchasing key components, B&O gains access to the suppliers' construction and development competences, without actually having the same qualifications. B&O often invests specifically in interfaces between key components and the other components in a product. In this manner, a certain degree of dependency is developed upon key suppliers. Single sourcing is often the case. Relationships between B&O and key suppliers are always based on cooperation agreements, in which technology, product, and operations relations are clearly defined and established. B&O has access to the suppliers' roadmaps for technology development. A Relations Committee is appointed with participation from the top management of both parties, which meets at least once a year. The relationships are evaluated at least once annually. In the event that performance deviations occur, immediate action is taken. If the pattern continues, management becomes involved.

System Suppliers

System suppliers invest along with B&O in their mutual relationship. A system supplier or a strategic supplier develops, in cooperation with B&O, a unique competence/component. The supplier could handle management and coordinating activities for the underlying supply chain and move assembly-ready subsystems forward. System suppliers contribute with processes, components, or systems, which are critical for the company's production processes, or they can compose a significant segment of the products' value. Cooperation with the company typically enables the vendor to become involved quite early on in the development of new products. For example, the supplier may quite feasibly be included in design and construction phases. The supplier is allowed online access to communication between the involved parties, sales forecasts, production plans, and advance material demand. Open calculations are a requirement. There are clearly defined boundaries between system suppliers and B&O. Top management from both parties meets at least once a year. Yearly production improvements are agreed upon within logistics, quality, and costs. This type of cooperation agreement is limited to relatively few suppliers, as its development and maintenance demand a large number of resources from both sides.

www.bang-olufsen.com

3. Strategic Implications of the SCM Concept

"No business is an island." All companies are involved in a network of relationships with other companies. Some relationships have strong bonds, while others do not. An industrial network is dynamic. That is to say, new relations develop and old ones dissolve. The individual company's success is dependent on, among other things, the ability to participate in these networks of business relationships.

The SCM concept's strategic perspective forms a basis for discerning the company's position in its network. Choosing the central SCM cooperation partners is also made easier through this identification process. Working together in a focused manner allows the network to secure the best possible support for the joint business strategy. Charles Fine (1998) explains:

> *A company is its chain of continually evolving capabilities – that is, its own capabilities plus the capabilities of everyone it does business with.*

The SCM concept also contributes methods by which a structure for future cooperation between chosen partners can secure development possibilities among actors in the supply chain.

The Competitive Situation

The market mechanisms between customers, competitors, and vendors have changed radically during the last decades. Increased globalisation and liberalisation of trade, shorter product life, and enhanced market segments, have all put pressure on businesses to reduce costs and decrease production time. Additional factors such as escalating consumer expectations of service and quality have also increased competitive pressure.

In most markets, the differences between the products' functional abilities are minimal, and can as a result seldom be used to differentiate the individual company from its competitors. It is the company's ability to provide service and to convert specific knowledge to increased performance, which can give the customer the feeling of increased value. A consistently high level of customer service is one of the central parameters of competition, and therefore one of the ways in which companies can differentiate themselves from competitors in future.

As a result, management must always seek new ways and means to re-establish competitive abilities and improve profitability. Interest in companies' suppliers, customers, and the way management chooses to position itself in relation to the network of suppliers, customers, and other cooperative partners, is increasing.

During the last 5-10 years many companies have worked towards making internal business processes more effective by restructuring in order to create a process-oriented framework, often supported by an IT system (ERP). The process orientation contributes to improving internal flows and creating transparency as well as to fostering a new perspective. With a better perspective on the company's internal processes, and thereby also the supply chain, management is strengthened in its ability to define which competences and resources the company should focus on in its increased cooperation with chosen network relations.

One of management's greatest challenges is often to create a connection between strategic visions and day-to-day operations. With regard to this challenge, the SCM concept can be used in conjunction with selecting, establishing, developing, and managing the chosen relationships, which are also the network potentials that support a given selected strategy. The concept encompasses strategic perspectives in connection with choosing SCM partners, as well as the achievement of a more operational approach to how cooperation in the relationship should develop through optimal positioning in the supply chain. The first step is to prioritise the use of resources in relation to the individual relationships in the network. The next step is to establish relationships and formulate goals for the chosen network participants.

There is considerable potential for cooperation in the establishment of structures throughout the supply chain, both internally and externally. Often, there are many activities that do not create value involved in trade between two companies. Jointly locating and eliminating these activities, as well as developing cooperative goals and guidelines for the future can focus resources on real improvements and development possibilities. This can lead to growth that not only reduce costs, but also improves quality and service.

The future scene of competition will increasingly be between networks. The individual company will not be able to achieve the necessary competitive strength alone in the market, but will be dependent on, and affected by, the network it functions as a part of.

SCM as a Value Generating Concept

During the start-up of an SCM project it can be difficult to document cost reduction. A preliminary analysis can help shed light on the potential for cost reduction between parts of the supply chain. Therefore, the development of a preliminary SCM analysis and the successive project are often based on common sense and educated guesses, which present themselves during the preliminary analysis. In order to be specific about the potential savings involved in SCM cooperation, it is a good idea to establish project groups that are representative of the different links in the supply chain. Through this type of communication, an understanding of each others' business processes arises, which is the first step towards identifying a number of focus areas, and thereby aspects for potential improvement.

Based on the pilot study, the potential for savings can be estimated in more concrete terms. The point here is to test other forms of cooperation, based on the assumption that it could be appropriate to do things differently. A classic example is Henry Ford's organisation of car production with the assembly line concept. To do things differently and to seek to eliminate activities that do not add value can increase competitive ability. There is a great difference between Ford's assembly line of 1914 and the SCM concept. The similarities are found in analysing the company's processes from a holistic or broad perspective, thinking untraditionally, and daring to test in practice new forms of cooperation.

Even though it is impossible to be specific about the benefits of a SCM solution during the start-up phase, experience shows that after the barriers are first broken down through dialogue and cooperation, a unique form of cooperation results between the partners. The cooperation that is developed between companies is a result of interaction between the individuals playing their respective roles in the integrated processes. A wholly new competence is built up in these employees, specifically the ability to cooperate and communicate across functions and company boundaries. This competence is difficult for competitors to understand and to copy.

Competitive Advantage through SCM

This section gives examples of the benefits companies realise through implementation of the SCM concept. It is especially important during the implementation phase to discuss internally the advantages that the company seeks to achieve, thereby clarifying what the motivation is for focusing on supply chain efficiency as well as better use of the company's network.

A condition for achieving considerable benefits through SCM cooperation is that the company has coordinated its own internal processes, as well as having made them efficient. If this preliminary work has not been completed, then the company will often not be prepared to enter into a closer form of cooperation with the other participants in the supply chain. Nor will the company be able to define the areas of real possibility for improvement, as identified in relation to customers, vendors, and other network relations. Quite simply stated, this is the principle of "taking care of your own business first."

Benefits of the SCM Concept

The benefits that can be achieved by implementing the SCM concept often presuppose that the supply chain be redesigned from scratch, and is reconstructed so that the focus is centred around changing the cost structure, rather than mere "cost cutting".

Benefits that are often mentioned in connection with SCM include:
- Increased flexibility towards the customers' wishes
- Quicker and more precise delivery time
- Greater customer loyalty and resulting increase in sales
- Fewer backorders/sold out situations
- Reduced total costs
- Motivated and focused vendors

Customer-driven Supply Chains
The trend in many industries is towards "mass customisation." This type of production is tailored to the individual needs of the customer, and the production system is geared towards effective production and finishing processes, which can quickly be changed from one product type to another. The production form necessitates very close cooperation between the parties involved in the supply chain. As production is controlled by customer orders, a finished product

inventory exists only to a very limited degree. On the other hand, this process can prepare the individual customer orders by building up a component and standard product inventory, which can later be utilised in the assembly process when a customer order has been received. Another solution is to enter into partnership agreements with suppliers regarding delivery according to an agreed max-min framework. This solution is also referred to as the vendor managed inventory (VMI), or automatic replenishment. A third possibility is "just-in-time" deliveries from suppliers, with deliveries occurring within narrow "time windows" in an order that allows for the components to enter directly into the assembly process (synchronised supply).

More Responsive Supply Chains

Short lead times and precision delivery are important parameters of competition. The short lead time is necessary in order to reduce inventory binding throughout the supply chain and to limit the risk of having out-of-date products. The shorter the lead-time, the less capital is bound up in safety and dispatch inventories. Delivery precision is also important because it is a prerequisite for customers being able to reduce their safety inventories, as well as for living up to delivery agreements with their customers.

The influence of quick and precise delivery becomes clear in the car industry, as there are many suppliers bound by just-in-time agreements with the producers, and where the frequency of delivery is high. At the same time the "time window" between ordering and delivery is often just a few hours. This time-based aspect of competition is also crucial in other industries. A Similar degree of importance is found in the food product, electronic, and pharmaceutical industries.

One of the reasons why Dell Computers is such a big success is that Dell has built up their assembly and delivery structure so that they can provide a customer specific computer within five days in most of Europe. Benetton can, within seven days, replenish fashion clothes from their distribution centre in Italy to a store USA. The successful Spanish apparel retailing chain Zara is able to deliver fashion garments to stores in Europe within 24 hours and in Japan within 48-72 hours. B&O is prepared to deliver a customized audio/video system to anywhere in Europe within five days. Spareparts can be received by B&O dealers and repair shops in Europe within 24 hours after ordering, because of a partnership agreement B&O has with an international express carrier.

Greater Customer Loyalty and Resulting Increase in Sales

One of the fringe benefits of close customer cooperation is a higher degree of customer loyalty. By building up long-term, trust-based cooperation with one's key customers, several things fall into place. First, the risk of the customer choosing another, slightly cheaper supplier diminishes. This risk becomes smaller because of the other benefits of the established cooperation, for example, quick and precise delivery, high quality, simplified administration, and lower quality control costs. The customer's purchasing budget can as a result show lower total costs. In addition, there are strong possibilities for increasing sales with the customer if the customer increases their assortment or market area.

Fewer Backorders/Sold Out Situations

Through closer cooperation among the actors in the whole supply chain, it is possible to reduce backorders and sold out situations. The rapid and open information exchange between involved parties allows vendors to plan their purchasing and production earlier, and thereby react more quickly to changes in demand. Instead of relying on uncertain sales forecasts, the supplier can directly calculate the future need for materials and products. This situation is based on the condition that customers are willing to provide their cooperative partners with information about actual sales figures, inventories, and planned sales campaigns.

Reduced Total Costs

Examples of areas in which the total supply chain costs can be reduced include:

- Elimination of double inspections – for example, receiving goods and quality control for the customer. If there is close, long-term cooperation with key vendors, it is possible to reduce or completely eliminate quality inspection functions, which in reality is a consequence of not trusting the other party. Often receiving check, invoice control etc. is more reflections of habit than of necessity. If the supplier is more closely connected to the customer company through partnership agreements, then a number of control functions can be eliminated. As a result, savings in terms of both cost and time can be achieved.

- Reduction of the total inventory can result from shorter lead times and more precise planning. The greater the understanding an individual company in a supply chain has of its future sales, the less necessary it is to have safety stock in case of changes in sales. As forecasts and sales expectations become generally unstable the longer into the future they are estimated, a limited lead time, in and of itself, will increase the reliability of the sales forecasts.

- Better capacity utilisation through improved planning and fewer rush orders. If a producer can plan its purchasing and production in good time, the production costs, all else equal, will be reduced, benefiting all involved parties. B&O allows key vendors access to a system that shows B&O's need for materials and components, with good advance notice. This allows suppliers to plan their purchasing and production much more accurately than if they were to wait for purchasing orders from B&O.

Motivated and Focused Suppliers
One of the benefits of entering into close, long-term cooperation with key suppliers is that the suppliers see themselves as a continuation of the customer company. In a traditional "arm's length" relationship, which is based on mutual distrust, and for which prices are often the most important parameter, vendors often spend too many resources on working up offers. These offers are often only partially realised, or only go through if the price is so low that there is no possibility for profit. In the long term this process is exhausting for all parties, and in the end, an unproductive use of resources.

The Cooperation between B&O, Kaiserplast, and WBL
Kaiserplast is a vendor of injected mould plastic components. WBL produces injected forms for Kaiserplast's injected mould machines. Kaiserplast has for many years delivered injected mould components to B&O, but as a capacity supplier and in competition with other injected mould producers. B&O typically obtained bids from 4-5 suppliers, before they chose a vendor. In the same manner, Kaiserplast got quotes from different producers of injected forms and tools. The result was that Kaiserplast and WBL spent both time and resources on generating offers and calculations, without having any guarantee that the order would eventually be placed with them.

In 1997 B&O entered into a partnership agreement with Kaiserplast. At the same time Kaiserplast took over a portion of B&O's injected form machines, as well as some of B&O's employees from the department that had been closed. The new cooperation agreement represented a dramatic change in the relationship between B&O and Kaiserplast. From being a standard component vendor during a period when B&O's own capacity was completely full, Kaiserplast became an integrated part of B&O's production process. Technicians from Kaiserplast were successively involved in product development and invited to internal B&O seminars.

This close cooperation between B&O and Kaiserplast also affected cooperative relationships with the tool and injected form producer, WBL. Previously, B&O and Kaiserplast had only used WBL as a supplier when the opportunity presented itself. This relationship changed so that there was a day-to-day connection, where B&O, Kaiserplast and WBL continuously developed new injected forms and tools in close cooperation. All three parties benefited from this change in attitude towards cooperation. B&O got better quality for the same price, whereas Kaiserplast and WBL could concentrate on quality and product development, instead of generating offers.

Principles for Managing Supply Chains

In this section the important management principles in supply chains will be outlined. The first topic concerns working on the basis of customers' orders rather than starting with forecasts. This aspect is referred to as the postponement principle. The second topic focuses on "transparency" (sharing of information) in the supply chain. This approach is referred to as the whiplash effect or bullwhip effect.

Postponement

Future development points in the direction of mass customisation. This means that production is customised, the production facilities are set up for greater efficiency, and final assembly can easily change from one product line to another.

This form of production demands very close interaction between parties along the entire supply chain. As the production is controlled by the customers' orders it is difficult for the company to have a finished inventory waiting. On the other hand, the company can prepare for the production of individual customer orders by building a stock of components and standard goods, which can all enter the final assembly process, when the actual customer order is received.

Customised production is based on two main principles that are closely connected. The first is modularisation and the second is postponement. Modularisation refers to a finished product being prepared and individualised from different components with a well-defined interface. By combining the components to satisfy the customers' needs for specific products, it is possible to manufacture a large number of different products with a limited number of components. The customer can, for example, order a PC comprising parts selected from a number of choices of hard discs, processors, control systems, software, screens, and a variety of accessories. The finished customer orders appear as individualised orders with unique capabilities, but are in reality manufactured with a number of standard components.

Furthermore, modularisation has the advantage that each component supplier has the possibility of defining product development of its specific component, without affecting the other components. Thus, within the past 15 years, Intel has developed a number of new versions of processors from version 286 to Pentium 4. Microsoft has developed new Windows programmes and office programme packages. Seagate has developed a number of new discs and CD-ROM drivers. Modularisation also means that the competition within the different component areas is increasing, as is the demand for speedier product development.

In the 1970's large integrated computer manufacturers dominated the computer industry, with IBM in the lead. Compatibility between manufacturers was very limited: people were either IBM users or Digital Equipment users. During the 1980's IBM had to give up the integrated product configuration, and started the production of a modularized PC. This decision meant that a number of new competitors entered the market, taking market shares from IBM and other large computer manufacturers. In 2004 IBM sold its PC production to the Chinese PC producer Lenovo.

Postponement (Pagh & Cooper, 1998) is an important principle in the design of the supply chain because it can reduce uncertainty as well as costs in relation to capital tied up in finished goods inventories.

There are three different postponement strategies:
1. Production postponement
2. Distribution postponement
3. Full postponement

The production postponement strategy means delaying the actual customisation of the product until the customer order is received. The customisation may, for example, be the final assembly stage of the product, the packaging, price tagging, and country marking. Instead of having a stock full of finished products for a specific customer group, or market area, the manufacturer can stock generic products that can be used for different customers and market areas.

A well-known example is Hewlett-Packard's customisation of DeskJet printers. Here manuals, electrical plugs, and wrapping are added to the generic version of the DeskJet at each distribution centre when the specific order is received. HP can thus transport in bulk to regional distributions centres, and thereby achieve scale advantages in production and transportation. At the same time, HP avoids having a stock of costly goods that can only be sold in specific markets.

The production postponement strategy is shown in Figure 3.1.

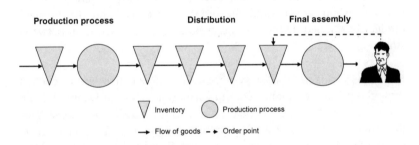

Figure 3.1 Production postponement

The distribution postponement strategy refers to distributing the product directly to the customers from a central warehouse. The products are finished when they are placed in the warehouse. The advantage of using distribution postponement is that the finished products can be directed to different customers or markets according to the actual demand. Atlas Copco Tools use this strategy. Their products are transported directly from the different factories to a European distribution centre. From here, the products are sent directly to the customers.

The distribution postponement strategy is shown in Figure 3.2.

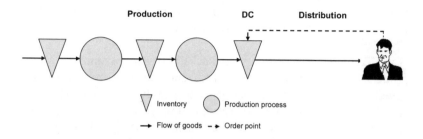

Figure 3.2 Distribution postponement

The full postponement strategy is a combination of the two strategies described above. In full postponement, the customisation of the products is postponed until the order is received, and the finished product is shipped directly to the customer, without using in-between storage.

B&O has changed from a system with national distribution centres throughout Europe, to one central distribution centre in Denmark from where the products are shipped directly to the dealers, and sometimes directly to the final customers. Through this process, B&O saves costs in stock binding, because less safety stock is needed for one centralised stock than for e.g. 15 national warehouses. At the same time, the situation of being sold out in one country while having too many goods in another country is avoided. It is also much easier to ensure efficient stock control and stock handling in one centralised warehouse.

The full postponement strategy is shown in Figure 3.3.

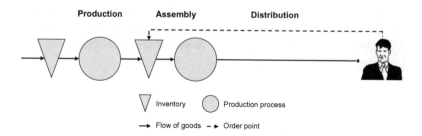

Figure 3.3 Full postponement

The Whiplash Effect

In a traditional supply chain, information about the final customer's actual demand is often delayed from one link in the supply chain to the next. This phenomenon is often called the whiplash effect (Hau Lee, 1997) or the Forrester effect. Each link in the supply chain will often have its own system for distributing and organising based on the information it receives from the subsequent link in the supply chain. The vendor will purchase and produce on the basis of incoming orders from the producer. The producer will arrange its activities depending on the orders received from the wholesaler. The wholesaler will reorder as necessary based on the orders from the retailer. The retailer will place their orders based on the behavioural demand patterns of the final customer. All links in the supply chain will have their own built-in ordering routines, which are based on reorder points and quantities. This practice creates larger fluctuations in the demand, the further upwards the supply chain one comes. The effect is illustrated in Figure 3.4.

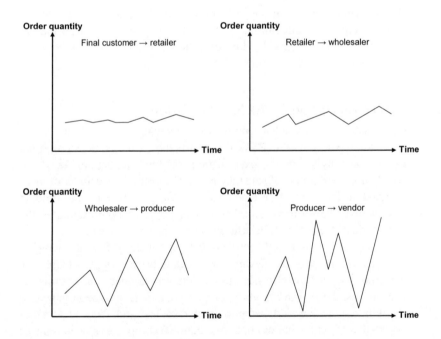

Figure 3.4 The Whiplash Effect

The whiplash effect can have other causes than insufficient information between links in the supply chain, including:

- Shipment consolidation, in order to achieve better distribution capacity utilisation.
- Order consolidation, in order to attain quantity discounts or to simplify ordering.
- Sales campaigns, which can encourage customers to purchase in larger quantities than they actually need. This tendency can give an incorrect impression of demand.
- Speculation in shortage situations, which leads customers to order more than they need in the hope of securing a larger percentage of the allocated products.
- Delays as a result of administrative routines, for example weekly ordering or long transport times (for example, container transport from the Far East).

By exchanging information on forecasts, production plans, inventory, and principles of allocation, as well as by integrating information systems between the involved parties, the unfortunate consequences of large fluctuations in demand can be reduced considerably.

Tax Optimisation in the Supply Chain

Optimisation and complete control of a company's supply chain must also take into account the physical infrastructure. This can be exemplified by a company's critical examination of the number of factories, warehouses, and points of sale they have. The optimal placement of these physical attributes must be determined if effective material and product flows are to be ensured. Another key example of optimisation is the evaluation of the potential benefit of using a shared service centre.

For companies that sell their products in several different countries, tax-oriented analysis is relevant with regard to the supply chain. The company's legal flow also has implications for earnings and optimising. It is not just the improvements a company can achieve through increased flexibility - quicker and better market response and reduced logistics costs - that affect the bottom line. International companies should think of tax costs as a controllable cost, on the same level as other costs in the supply chain. It is quite feasible to improve the bottom line result by reducing costs, an effect that can be achieved by optimising the legal units in a supply chain. Take as an example a company that expects to achieve a 10% savings on their European production locations over the next four years through optimisation of the supply chain. If these savings can be channelled into a legal unit in a country with low taxes, the company can reduce the taxation of the increased earnings.

By including tax-technical considerations in the design or restructuring of a company's physical supply chain, factories can be placed where advantages are greatest, both from a cost-savings point of view, and a tax-savings point of view.

Tax Optimising

A parent company is typically located in the country where the founder lives and works. Over time several factories, distribution centres, and sales offices may be established in various other countries, which often function as independent legal units.

Looking at the supply chain from a tax-oriented perspective, a legal unit is established directly under the parent company (a principal). The principal serves as the central unit in the business. In this way, the activities are controlled and coordinated in the factories by buying production facilities on a contract basis, hiring sales agents who handle the customers, and by controlling and owning stock items ranging from raw materials to the finished products. In principle, all legal flows go through the parent company, as illustrated in Figure 3.5.

Material and product flows go from the vendor, via production, to the distribution centres. The companies in each country are responsible for the national customers, and the customers can place their orders directly with the local sales team, a call centre, or through an e-business channel.

The flow of information has thus been changed so that plans for demand, and sales orders, all pass through the principal. The principal is the central organisation that "owns" the supply chain and thereby does all the planning including stock control, production planning, and administration of the vendors.

In order to create the best possible tax structure conditions, it is necessary for the principal to have full ownership of the raw components, from the time they are received from the vendor, throughout the entire production process and until the finished products can be delivered to the customers. The principal buys the production process, and the production unit does not own the product, just as is the case when a company uses a subcontractor. In this way the largest portion of the earnings is placed in the hands of the principal. If the homeland of the principal has lower taxes than the country in which the production unit is located, the net result will be better on the bottom line.

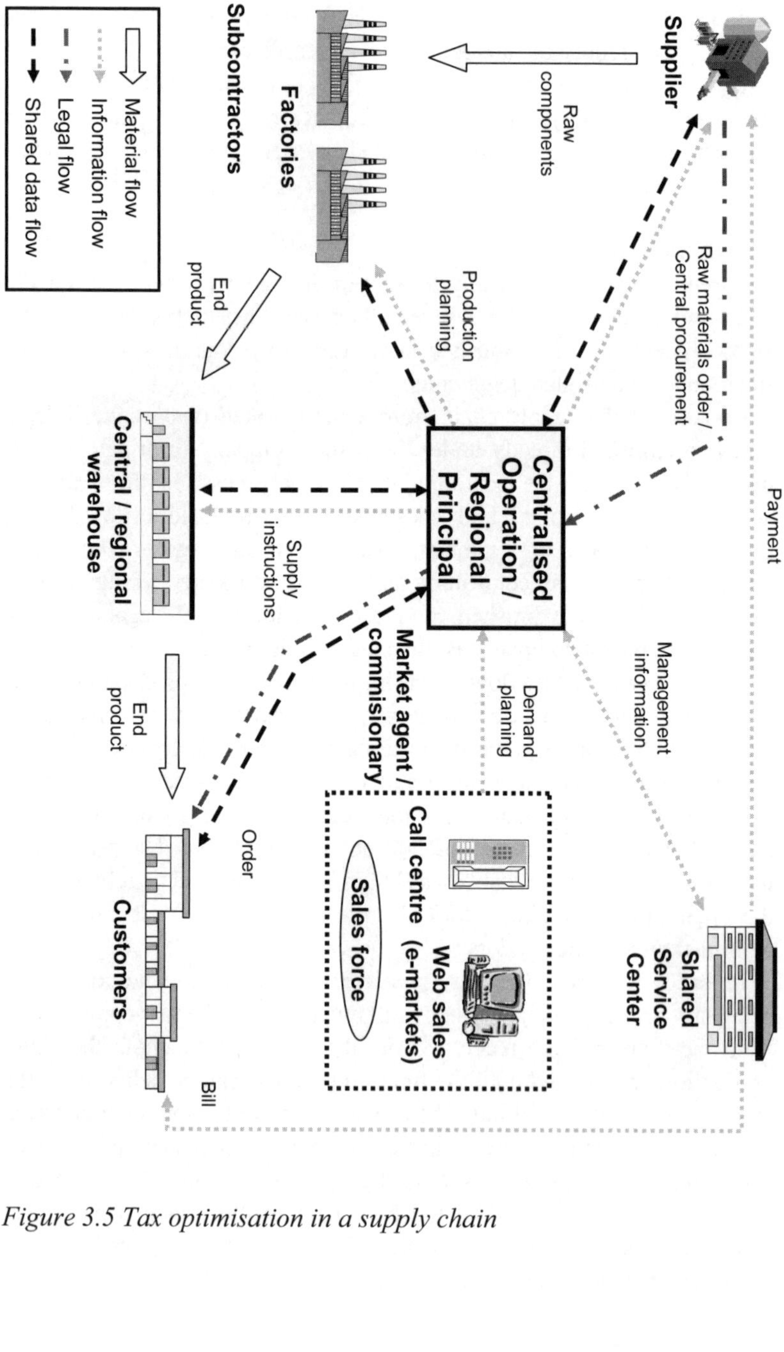

Figure 3.5 Tax optimisation in a supply chain

The company's earning structure will be split, so that the production and sales units achieve a profit by producing, and sales commissions are held locally. The growth in earnings from production and sales goes to the principal, as shown in Figure 3.6.

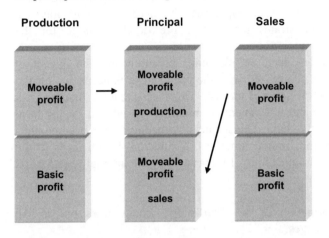

Figure 3.6 Profit sharing between principal and agent

Tax advantages are achieved by:
- Identifying and establishing a principal structure in a country with a favourable tax level.
- Transferring as much as possible of the earnings created in the supply chain to the principal.
- Minimising functions, assets, risks, and thereby earnings in countries with high taxation.

One of the determination factors for achieving tax advantages is that the principal must have substance, which means that it is not sufficient to establish a fictive office in a country with low taxes. The principal must execute the administrative and planning activities in order to be able to justify its earnings. It also means that the largest part of the risks must be moved from the local units to the principal, to achieve balance between profit and risk.

Implications of using tax optimising
It is only possible to realise tax savings if a structure is created in the supply chain that reflects the new situation. New contracts with vendors must therefore be signed, as the company also needs to physically relocate central decision makers to the principal.

The demand for substance where the principal is situated makes it necessary to centralise units related to planning, procurement, marketing, and HQ functions. Additionally, the relocation of key resources from the physical production, distribution, and sales units to the location of the principal may be necessary. This physical reshuffling demonstrates the real nature of the change for the business.

When activities such as planning, procurement, and inventory management are centralised with the principal, it is necessary for the principal to assume some of the risk. This means that the financial risk related to assets and investments in buildings is reduced for the local units in the supply chain. This means that the local units become units with low risk and limited functions, a situation, which leads to the transferring the implications of power within the internal organisation structure.

A tax transformation of the total supply chain gives rise to the following challenges:

- Restructuring of the organisation. When the key decision makers are relocated the regional headquarters are left with less strategic tasks. These will naturally go to the principal where the power is centralised. This could very well lead to resistance from powerful decision makers within the local units.
- Restructuring of the supply chain from a traditional functional orientation to a process orientation with focus on the total supply chain. This leads to a change in structure from being divided by countries, to being divided by regions.
- System integration between the different units is a necessity in order to be able to cope with the large amounts of data and information that flow between the units and to support standardised and robust processes.
- Massive demand for resources to coordinate and alter the supply chain.
- Securing the full ownership of raw materials, work-in-process, and finished goods by the principal until delivery to the customer. This can only be ensured by having an appropriate IT system and a solid flow structure.

Following restructuring on the basis of a tax-oriented perspective, responsibilities are split between the local offices and the principal in a new way, as shown in Table 3.1.

Responsibility	Before Restructuring	After Restructuring
Who owns the inventory?	Local	Central planning / Principal
Who owns the customer?	Local	Local
Who makes the decisions regarding inventory and replenishment?	Local	Principal
Who decides what to order from the vendors?	Local	Principal
Who decides what is to be manufactured?	Local	Principal
Where is the support unit placed?	Local	Shared Service Centre
Who is responsible for profit?	Local	Regional management

Table 3.1 Responsibility split between principal and local office before and after restructuring

Resistance from the local management

The simultaneous restructuring of both the roles of players and power often leads to a situation in which people present the biggest challenges and barriers to change. This resistance comes especially from the senior management of local units. For the local units restructuring entails a serious reduction in the influence and importance of local management. Therefore, as an important part of the process, a solid and focused change management effort is necessary.

Is the company ready for a tax transformation?

To be able to exploit the extra tax advantages and thereby restructuring of the legal flow, the supply chain must be optimised and well structured. The tax optimisation made possible by establishing a principal should be seen as an extra advantage that can be achieved when the company has structured and optimised its supply chain.

This means that, among other things, the following steps must be followed:

- A production strategy must be formulated
- A decision must be made regarding how many production facilities, distribution centres, and sales units are optimal for the company's value and supply chain.
- The vendor base must be reduced and a decision must be made regarding the desired level of cooperation with different types of vendors.
- Shared standard procedures for key processes must be implemented.
- A shared service centre and call centre should probably be established.
- A shared ERP system should be established, which ensures the easy flow of information across the internal supply chain.
- It must be made clear what financial factors are driving the extended supply chain.

It is clearly a major task for management and the organisation as a whole to optimise and restructure the supply chain in order to realise extra tax savings. In some companies the tax potential has been part of a business case for restructuring and optimising of the supply chain.

4. Process Orientation and Relationship Management

The SCM concept, with its overall perspective on the supply chain, has been difficult for many companies to operationalise. Seen from an operational level, the complexity of the SCM concept is so vast that it is necessary to break down the supply chain into smaller segments (dyads) in order to understand it. This does not mean that the overall perspective is thrown aside, but rather that it must be looked at as a way to create a foundation for realising the vision and perspectives of the SCM concept.

In recent years, new terms have arisen which build upon the same basic ideas as the SCM concept. These terms focus more on two-sided relationships (dyads) with customers or suppliers. Supplier Relationship Management (SRM), Customer Relationship Management (CRM), Vendor Management Inventory (VMI), and ECR/CPFR are among the most recent concepts.

Besides focusing on relations in the external supply chain, companies also need to focus on the internal supply chain and on their organisation structure. Many companies are already actively engaged in this exercise, which is often linked to the implementation of a shared IT system. In the first section below, the question of function or process orientation will be discussed, before turning to a consideration of how external relationships can be controlled. The chapter as a whole deals with the different focus areas and forms of cooperation that can be seen as prerequisites for making the SCM concept work.

Function or Process Orientation

Focus in a function-oriented company is on managing, controlling and measuring the activities bound to a specific function. Budgets, accounts, critical success factors, and award systems are set for each functional area. Each department is driven by a budget, which it must fulfil for a given period. When a department has reached its budget target, whether it is based on costs, resources, or earnings, it has performed well and will be rewarded.

A line manager, who will often see his/her area of responsibility as his/her "kingdom" where nobody else should interfere, manages each function. Attempts to work across a function-oriented company will lead to resistance from managers guarding their territory, who do not want to empower or leave decisions to others within the organisation. The worse case scenario, in the eyes of these managers, would be having control or decision-making lying in the hands of companies external to the organisation.

The division of a company according to functions does have its advantages when the aim is to exploit specialised knowledge and experience within different areas. There may be disadvantages, however, if the aim is to gain an overall understanding of the company and develop a process orientation. There is a strong risk that each department will sub-optimise from the perspective of the company as a whole. For example, the procurement department may focus on discounts and low prices, the production department typically tries to ensure a high utilisation of the production capacity and low cost per unit produced, and the sales department is concerned with keeping abreast of market news and ensuring that there are many products to choose from, and a high level of service for all customers.

These built-in conflicts and opposing targets are well known to most managers, but hard to avoid in the day-to-day life of the company. The risk of sub-optimisation similarly increases when each company within the supply chain works towards optimising its own internal business processes only, rather than looking at the supply chain as a whole.

A number of companies have realised the need to change their vertical organisation structure to a more horisontal structure. This change draws attention to processes, as opposed to looking at the functional barriers and the different steps of the supply chain. Setting up a working process management is a major challenge for management, as it requires the ability to predict organisational changes, and to establish new management forms, decision-making methods, tasks, and award systems.

Some of the central issues, which need to be addressed, include:

- Who should be responsible for the selected processes?
- What is the best way of measuring the process?
- How should the company be organised in order to support the processes?

Process management may consist of "main process owners" of each of the main processes within the company, together with a number of "sub process owners" for each of the main processes' sub processes. A part of the management team is responsible for managing and developing the main process and sub processes. The main process owner may be part of a higher decision group, together with the top management and line managers who coordinate the main processes. The various roles are shown in Figure 4.1.

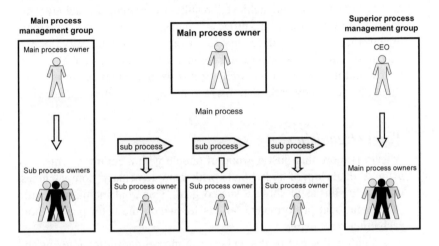

Figure 4.1 Process Management
Source: Ambeck & Beyer (2000)

The owner of the main process is responsible for coordination of the main process, e.g. order fulfilment from ordering through to delivery to the customer. Coordination must take place in close cooperation with the owners of the individual processes. The owner of the main process should have a relatively top-level position within the organisation, so that he/she is able to influence the line functions, which the processes pass through.

The owner of a specific individual process is responsible for coordinating the activities that go on in each department where the process is executed. The owner of the individual process must be centrally placed in conjunction with the individual process, but not be responsible for deciding how the individual process is to be carried out. This responsibility rests on the line manager's shoulders.

The owners of the main processes, the owners of the individual processes, and the line management are all part of a decision group that takes care of the overall main process. This superior process management group looks at ongoing improvements and the daily work of the company and makes decisions concerning the coordination of daily tasks for all main processes. The group also decides whether or not there is a need for new resources for some of the main processes, and whether or not the time prioritisation is appropriate for each task.

It is important to work out visible and operational targets, budgets, and success factors for each process. Moreover, continuous follow-up on the set targets, and achieved results, is crucial. To achieve the desired results from a process manager within a functional organisation, it is also necessary to let the process perspective play a part in the company's reward and compensation systems, collaboration forms, and management hierarchy. Rewards and achievement of goals should be guided by process terms, and not by each individual activity.

Team Organising

A team is more than just a group of people with a common project. A team is made up of individuals with complementary competencies, who are enthusiastic about a shared goal. This goal includes specific and operational performance targets for which the team players hold each other responsible.

A dividing line can be drawn between intra-organisational teams and inter-organisational teams. Teams of employees from sales/marketing, logistics, production, and accounting can exemplify intra-organisational teams. This type of team is necessary in order to establish a process thinking in a company in order to coordinate activities across line functions. Inter-organisational teams are composed of representatives from different companies in the supply chain. These teams are important connection points between the supply chain participants.

Teams and other organisational forms that are designed to promote cooperation across functions and companies should be supplemented with incentive programmes that reward the total efforts of the team. If wages and career possibilities continue to be based on individual performance and competition, then employees cannot be expected to put themselves wholeheartedly into teamwork.

It is also important that team goals are well defined, operational, and directly related to the company's overall goal/vision. If this is not the case, then good results cannot be anticipated from the team's efforts. Correspondingly, it is important that a company's overall vision and goals are articulated clearly, so that the challenges of fulfilling the described goals are clear to each team member.

Relationship Management

The old saying, "show me your friends and I will tell you who you are" holds true in the business world. A company's ability to build the right relationships today is a factor in determining its level of competitiveness. This reality is supported by the increasing interest in the idea of controlling relationships and exchanging information. By focusing resources on cooperative partners of strategic importance, a need for relationship efficiency with other parties arises, and as a result the total transaction costs can be reduced.

Based on this situation, a change can be observed in the way relationships between companies are managed. Whereas previously, a one-to-one relationship was common between a customer's purchasing department and the supplier's sales department, today, focus is increasingly placed on the integration of several processes in order to improve the total value of a supply chain.

With closer collaboration between the chosen processes, costs related to companies' communications could increase. This increase can be avoided by concentrating on efficiency of communication and prioritising in accordance with the importance of the relationship for the individual company.

Therefore, there is also an increasing interest in concepts and tools that support and structure the flow of such relations. During the last decade, the SCM concept has contributed to emphasising the need for controlling the supply chain, as well as for closer integration between businesses. The next step is realising some of the benefits beyond the optimisation of the, material, and information flows.

SRM, CRM, VMI, ECR/CPFR are all characteristic of the fundamental thought processes behind the SCM concept, and support the integration of selected processes between companies in the supply chain. These management foci can also support different IT platforms, which in turn make it possible to manage and systematise relationships so that a greater degree of transparency is created for all links in the supply chain.

Supplier Relationship Management (SRM)

The potential cost savings to be gained through better strategic sourcing and supply chain execution are enormous and can significantly impact a company's competitive position.[5]

There is increasing focus on outsourcing, reduction of one's vendor base, as well as development of partnerships with the company's key suppliers. These factors, coupled with the company's increased awareness of optimising the flows of the supply chain, relation management, and integration between companies, creates an overall basis for the SRM concept.

SRM is not just about purchasing and strategic sourcing, but also includes creating, managing, and supporting relations to the suppliers. The goal is to establish sustainable improvement of the total supply chain from vendor to final customer.

In this section, the focus will primarily be the establishment and management of vendor relations, as well as the costs and benefits associated with SRM. However, the more traditional purchasing activities also encompassed by the SRM concept will only be discussed to a limited extent.

The creation of partnerships is often emphasised as the way to improve the efficiency of a supply chain. Attention is increasingly directed towards improved management of relationships with vendors in order to reduce prices and transaction costs, in part by putting the suppliers' competencies and knowledge to better use.

Improvements on the supply side can benefit a company's success, but the connection between vendor management and these improvements is often complex. Good, close supplier relations have become part of the proposed solution in connection with improving the supply chain. However, how good, close relations can be defined, and how the value of such relations is derived, are questions that often remain for a company's management and the purchasing department.

The reason for this uncertainty can be that many companies do not focus enough on the work that goes into preparing to enter into closer relations with vendors, as well as the on-going follow-up and development necessary for these relations. Additionally, there is a tendency to focus on the vendor instead of on the relationship and the related processes. It is generally believed that relationships in the

---

[5] Pierre Mitchell, Senior Analyst, AMR research, 2001

supply chain are generic, but in reality, there is a high level of specificity from relationship to relationship.

Working strategically and operationally with relationship management is a completely new area and way of thinking for most companies. Therefore, it is necessary to analyse how closer relations to the chosen vendors will affect the rest of the business, how a closer integration of the chosen processes can support the business strategy and the operational goals, and what the desired effect of entering into these relations is. In addition, the manner in which the suppliers are chosen and how the relationship is established and developed, are also key factors for consideration. After these topics have been thought through, the challenge remains of running and managing the relationships, as well as ensuring that the expected advantages are achieved.

Regardless of the level of integration in a relationship, there will always be both costs and benefits associated with it. By reducing the number of suppliers and establishing a closer relation to the chosen suppliers, the natural goal is to reduce the total relation costs and increase value creation.

Relation costs can be divided into two main areas:

Direct purchasing costs, which include the paid price for materials, logistics and transportation costs, as well as the administrative costs (transaction costs) associated with ordering/invoicing. These costs have also previously been focus areas for purchasing departments.

Relation costs are the costs connected with activities, which are necessary for the development and maintenance of a relationship. These costs can again be divided into two types. Establishing an account and managing the supplier in the internal administrative system can, for example generate costs that can be related to a specific supplier. Other examples may include: training/developing the supplier as well as solving problems or complications that arise in the relationship. The other cost type is related to supplier evaluation, inspection visits to the supplier, and analysis of the supplier alternatives. The latter costs are difficult to divide up and distribute in terms of the individual vendor, but they decrease as the number of suppliers decreases.

Benefits

Benefits in SRM are gains that can be attributed to a closer connection with suppliers, thereby increasing transparency in the supply chain. Savings and other benefits can include: lower production costs, reduced R&D costs, decreased time-to-market, improved material flow and delivery time, and reduction of administrative costs. These savings can be achieved by developing a better understanding of each other's processes, increased integration, and exchange of knowledge and resources. However, it is often difficult to document that it is an increased focus on vendor relationships that has lead to the specified improvements.

In order to make close cooperation attractive for the parties involved, it is important that the benefits achieved are significantly greater than the costs incurred. As it is difficult to measure the resulting savings in concrete terms, top management in the companies involved should assess the qualitative and quantitative benefits that can be expected to result from closer cooperation.

Some benefits, which can result from closer cooperation with a supplier:
- Reduction of transaction costs by automating and simplifying the purchasing process.
- Increased quality, service, and supply reliability, as a result of better communication and greater understanding of the total process.
- Better utilisation of the supplier's competences and knowledge, through, for example, shared product development projects.
- Joint goals and visions for future collaboration.

In contrast to the SCM concept, the SRM concept creates a method of focusing on supplier management, whereby closer vendor relations can be operationalised. According to the traditional purchasing perception of suppliers, the primary goal is to maximise price savings. SRM, on the other hand, presents a base to manage the total vendor base effectively. In this way, the goal becomes focused on creating the right relations to the correctly chosen suppliers, establishing integrated processes, which support the relationship and the strategy for that area of business. There is also emphasis on generating appropriate internal organisational structure, competences, and attitudes.

Strategic and operational foci are both relevant in this context. A strategic focus can involve choosing and developing relations, and making the overall processes and policies for supply and purchasing concrete. An operational focus concentrates more on finding the best way to establish an appropriate form of cooperation and determining the possibilities for concrete improvements and initiatives.

Principles in SRM

In addition to choosing the right vendors and establishing the right relations, the SRM concept focuses primarily on three areas: information, cooperation, and integration. Supplier relations and purchasing processes are broken down to a greater degree than is the case in SCM. Integration of key activities related to the purchasing process is in focus. In this way, integration is seen as the driving force behind operationalising cooperation and exchanging information in the relationship with the vendors. The goal of implementing the SRM is, in much the same manner as is the case with the SCM concept, to create the "best fit" situation with suppliers through cooperation and information exchange in order to ensure a reduction in total costs in the supply chain, and to increase value for the consumer.

At the same time, from the customer company's perspective, focus is on the fact that SRM can result in optimisation of the purchasing functions. Some examples of this optimisation may include:

- Revising the supplier base and consolidating purchases.
- Optimising purchasing processes with the goal of reducing the total costs connected with purchasing. These costs include price, transaction costs, inventory costs etc.

Information

Getting the necessary and correct information at the right moment is crucial for participants in the supply chain, so that they can adjust and adapt their own activities to the needs of the entire supply chain. Therefore, one of the goals of information sharing is to create the possibility for collecting and sharing useful and accurate data, hereby increasing transparency in the supply chain. The data that is usually shared includes forecasts, historical data, market trends, production plans, as well as strategic information that affect partners in the supply chain. At the same time, there is an exchange of information related to individual transactions between the company and their vendors, including, for example, transferring of orders, order confirmations, and invoices.

Cooperation

The areas of cooperation with a supplier differ from supplier to supplier. In each individual relationship it is both necessary and important to evaluate the characteristics of cooperation as well as which business areas should be included. Processing orders, inventory, and shipping could be relevant categories for most cooperative relationships. On the other hand, joint design development, and product development, is far less frequently applicable.

The degree of closeness involved in cooperative arrangements depends on the number of processes the companies choose to integrate. This point alludes to the frame of reference for SCM in Chapter 2, where one of the focus areas in the three-component model is: "Which processes should be coupled to which relationships?"[6]

Integration

Through integration, a base for quick and precise exchange of information throughout the supply chain can be achieved. Based on the information that is shared among the actors, as well as the level of cooperation, the points of integration between companies are established. It is implicit in SRM that the customer company implements IT systems that support the purchasing process as well as the integration of the IT systems of the parties involved, enabling them to utilise a common communication platform.

The chosen form of cooperation, together with the level of information sharing and integration, is governed by the strategic nature of the product, and the fact of whether it is direct or indirect purchasing. This relationship is shown in Figure 4.2. The level of cooperation and number of contact points tend to be lower for vendors of indirect and non-strategic products.

---

[6] See also the B&O case for an application of a portfolio model for suppliers.

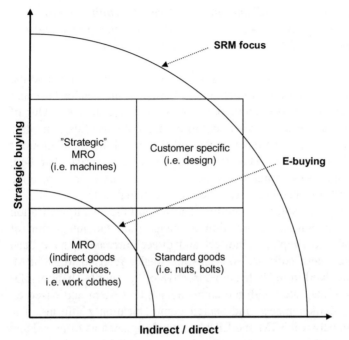

Figure 4.2 Portfolio Model for Purchasing

Purchasing of indirect and non-strategic products has traditionally required many resources relative to the importance of these products. Attention has increasingly been drawn to the optimisation and automatisation of the purchasing of these products. More and more companies have therefore begun to purchase these products through an electronic purchasing solution (e-Procurement). The goal of an e-procurement solution is to reduce the relationship costs per supplier and to release resources, which can be spent on direct purchasing, establishing closer cooperation, information exchange, and integration of the relevant processes. In other words, the goal has been to reduce the amount of time spent on routine purchasing tasks, so that there is more time to concentrate on strategic purchasing tasks.

IT tools that support SRM

*Supplier Relationship Management (SRM) is the process of **establishing, managing, and transacting** relationships, with suppliers' technology. SRM facilitates the **creation of value*** *through enhanced* **collaboration and supply chain execution,** *between enterprises and their key suppliers throughout the* **entire direct materials life cycle** *- from concept to delivery.[7]*

SRM emphasises the possibilities for controlling relationships and the integration of suppliers. An active monitoring of the vendor base and the relations to vendors can be both complicated and difficult. One of the reasons is that it is challenging to access and consolidate the data from different organisations that is needed to build the foundation for continued cooperation. Therefore, there is a greater risk that both strategic and operational discussions will be based on subjective feelings and educated guesses, rather than on actual facts.

In recent years, software solutions that support the operationalisation of close cooperation, information exchange, and the integration of customers' and suppliers' indirect and direct purchasing, have been developed. These software solutions are totally referred to as SRM, and are involved in the holistic perspective of the supply chain insofar as they are integrated with the company's ERP system and based on links to e-market places and shared communication platforms. The distinction between SRM and ERP is often designated as front end and back systems. This is a reference to the fact that SRM is in front of the firewall, whereas ERP is behind it.

SRM as an IT solution, in contrast to the more conceptual basis of the SCM concept, focuses primarily on the integration of the purchasing process and associated activities. Other processes that are relevant for specific suppliers, such as product development and production planning, are dealt with by other software solutions.[8]

The services that are included in the SRM module contribute to optimising both the company's internal and external purchasing processes.

Internal processes are addressed through systematic support of the purchasing process from bidding, ordering, receiving, and invoice approval, to contract control as well as analysis of purchasing data. In this manner, transaction costs can be reduced. Additionally, in most companies, a consolidated data foundation is created, which allows analyses and reports to be generated. These analyses and reports can be

---

[7] SAP, Presentation 2002

[8] See Chapter 5 on IT as a lever for deepening ERP. The implementation of an IT SRM solution presupposes that a company has analysed its vendor base, and gone through a strategic sourcing process.

used in negotiations with vendors, as well in conjunction with vendor/market evaluations. A better foundation of data increases the quality of supplier negotiations and thereby the possibility of reducing direct purchasing costs.

External processes come into play through electronic information exchange with suppliers. Placing/receiving orders, enquiries, giving/receiving estimates, and electronic invoicing are some examples of possible external information exchange processes, all of which reduce transaction costs. Integration of production planning and forecasting. are also possibilities, although this sort of information cannot be exchanged directly through the SRM concept, but must instead be drawn from the ERP system, which allows the vendor access.

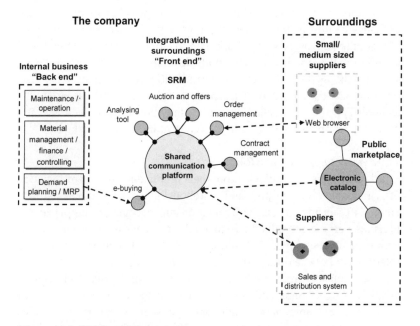

Figure 4.3 SRM model
Source: PwC Consulting, European Center of Excellence: SRM, presentation 2002

Figure 4.3 illustrates how a company today can systematically integrate with its surroundings, hereunder its vendors. "Back end" refers to the company's internal control system, which links to the surroundings through a shared communications platform (SRM

Exchange). In this way, the necessary exchange of information and the establishment of cooperation with regard to the optimising of purchasing processes become open possibilities for companies.

This description of the integration between a company and its surroundings is quite simplified. The real integration requires close cooperation, not just between the departments involved in the specified areas of business, but also between the IT departments in both companies.

Today, the largest ERP vendors offer a SRM module with all the functions necessary to support handling of the purchasing process and the possibility for integration via a shared communication platform. Typical functions include order management, purchasing module, auction module, contract control, and catalogue management.

IT support of supplier relations makes it possible to manage the exchange of information better and more cheaply than is possible with EDI solutions. However, it is important to emphasise the fact that there is substantial work involved in both developing a business strategy, and in making the necessary human relations flow smoothly. These relations are composed of 80% human effort and 20% information technology, though technology is often the necessary lever for handling the operational complexity inherent in the relationship.

Third party logistics and SRM

Third party logistics (TPL) is more than simple outsourcing of logistics activities, such as transport and warehousing, to an external partner. Here, TPL means "a long-term relationship between a shipper and a logistics service provider to render all or a considerable number of activities for the shipper" (Halldorsson & Skjoett-Larsen, 2004). The relationship between the parties is based on trust, a win-win situation, and willingness from both sides to solve problems and mutual adaptation of systems and organizations. In the case below, we will present an example of a relationship between a buyer of logistics services (Oticon) and a TPL provider (Wilson Logistics).

One-stop-logistics solution

Oticon is a managing hearing aid manufacturer. Oticon is a part of the Danish holding company, William Demant, which controls the following four business areas: Oticon, Bernafon, Diagnostic Instruments, and Personal Communication. The William Demant Holding (WDH) Group's revenue in 2003 was approximately 530 mills. Euro. The company has a total of 4,300 employees, of which almost 1,300 are employed in Denmark.

In 2001 the hearing aids business unit (Oticon and Bernafon) entered a one-stop shopping agreement with Wilson Logistics Group encompassing all inbound and outbound logistics activities globally, including spare parts. Five of the most prominent TPL providers represented in Denmark were invited to Oticon to present their visions, competencies, and proposals for solutions for the logistics team at Oticon. The selection was based on criteria, such as:

- Global coverage
- Advanced IT solutions
- Dedicated personnel and top management attention
- Buying power towards air freight companies

An important reason for choosing Wilson Logistics was that it had Scandinavian staff in most of its local offices, which eased communication. Another reason was that Oticon was considered a high priority as a key customer. For Oticon it was important that Wilson Logistics appointed their Vice MD in Denmark (from 2005 MD in Denmark) as the Global Account Manager for the Oticon agreement. This ensured top management commitment from the TPL provider on a global level. Oticon was ranked number five among the most important customers for Wilson Logistics. This also meant that the personnel in various airports and destinations would give a great deal of attention and high priority to Oticon's shipments. Costs were not the issue in the selection round. It was expected that if the TPL provider were able to meet the other requirements from Oticon, it would also be able to come up with competitive transport rates. The intention was to have a long-term partnership obliging both parties to eliminate all non-value activities, including the costs of controlling each other's operations.

The TPL contract runs for three years (renegotiated in 2004 for another three years) with annual renegotiations of rates and other conditions. At first, the TPL agreement encompassed only the hearing aids business unit (Oticon and Bernafon). However, the intention is eventually to extend the agreement to the other business units in the holding company, William Demant Holding Group. This transition has already taken place in several other business areas' sister companies, including FM equipment, Interacoustics, and the IT production in Glasgow. When other business units' sister companies join the agreement, they get the advantages of the global agreement, and rates that are calculated from William Demant's total volume. Oticon has a standard set up for all shipments, independent of their origin and destination.

Wilson Logistics is responsible for all the paperwork related to the shipments. They have established an Oticon Help Desk, which answers all inquiries from customers about the status of the shipments.

The TPL agreement is based on the 'open book' principle. Oticon pays according to the actual invoices Wilson receives from its subcontractors. In addition, Oticon pays a management fee. The size of the management fee depends on the actual turnover level and individual service offered. This is an incentive for Oticon to get as many companies as possible in the other business units to use the frame agreement. Oticon's capability of doing so is measured by Wilson. The task of persuading the sister companies to change from their current forwarder to Wilson cannot be done by force. Oticon uses the "ambassador principle" by encouraging satisfied users of the agreement to tell others about the advantages.

An important element in the partnership agreement is that Oticon informs Wilson about new activities, campaigns, product introductions, etc., so that Wilson can allocate specific resources to take care of shipments with high priority, and ensure space in aircraft.

In order to ensure that Wilson Logistics' services and rates can rival those of the best competitors, Oticon has asked Wilson Logistics to rank two of their closest competitors in the TPL market. These competitors could replace Wilson if there were a shift in TPL providers. During the year, the two providers are invited to Oticon to present their company and their points of view on future trends in the global transport market, and to discuss general matters within the transport market. Oticon, on their part, presents the company and its vision for the future. In this way, Oticon ensures that it has other alternatives besides Wilson Logistics, if something were to happen to their relationship, e.g. an acquisition from one of the dominant players in the TPL market. For Oticon, it is essential to be an important customer to the TPL provider. If, for example, Deutsche Post (DP) acquired Wilson, the focus would immediately be removed from Oticon. Instead of being a key customer, Oticon would turn into "Oti-who?". Oticon has tried to use DP, but changed again after two months because of the lack of focus placed on their partnership. Therefore, if Wilson is acquired by one of the global TPL providers, Oticon would reconsider its situation and possibly change to one of the two alternative TPL providers ranked by Wilson.

One drawback of one-stop shopping is that Oticon becomes dependent on one TPL provider and it might be difficult to change to another one. In order to avoid becoming too dependent on Wilson, Oticon has not bought or taken over any IT solutions from Wilson. However, the IT personnel from Oticon have agreed upon an IT platform and IT software in consultation with the IT personnel from Wilson. The information exchange between Oticon and Wilson is based on an EDI highway solution. Thus, Oticon can relatively easy change from one provider to another. Nevertheless, Oticon emphasises that they consider the partnership to be a long-term commitment.

Oticon's IT system is totally integrated with Wilson's. From Billund, Wilson can follow the packaging line at Oticon and the number of transport units packed. Wilson can see how many boxes there are in each shipment, and based on this information, they can prepare the shipment details and send shipment advice to the customers by e-mail or fax. When a shipment is completely packed, the information about the shipment (i.e. colli, cubic meters, weight) is send to Wilson in Billund together with the booking and the e-mail address or fax number of the customer. When Wilson receives all shipment details, it prepares the documents and bookings. Then Wilson's system automatically generates shipment advice, which is automatically sent to the customer with information about arrival time, airway bill number, etc. All of this information is automatically transmitted to Oticon's information system. There is no risk of mistakes or typing errors in the system. This also helps to keep non-value added activities at a minimum. The integrated information system between Wilson and Oticon shows Oticon's willingness to make changes in their system to gain mutual advantages.

Wilson's logistics services are measured along two dimensions: costs and performance. For each of the dimensions there are a number of KPI, which are measured regularly. The ten most important destinations (among them Glasgow, Newark, and Brisbane) account for about 50% of the measurements. Oticon focuses on the strategic points and tries to streamline the operations in these destinations.

The service requirements at Oticon differ for different product groups. As a general rule, the total lead time for ITE products is 5-7 days, and 24 hours for BTE products to Oticon sister companies and Oticon labs in Europe. Products from the central distribution centre in Thisted are picked up three times per day by courier companies and transported to Wilson's subsidiaries in Billund and Aalborg, where they are forwarded to their destinations by airfreight or express courier service in vans.

The agreement between Oticon and Wilson is based on a win-win situation. In the partnership agreement there is an obligation for both parties to take initiatives and to focus constantly on non-value-added activities. Wilson is under obligation to follow the development of the transport market very closely and select the most efficient subcontractors at any given time. In addition, they are under constant obligation to reduce costs and improve performance. Any savings made must be shared between the partners. For Oticon, the obligation is to roll out the frame agreements to other sister companies in William Demant Holding.

With regard to outsourcing, Oticon has only one person responsible for the transport operations. There are about 150 shipments per day. The same person is also responsible for communicating with the new companies in the agreement. Once a year a SWOT analysis is performed, which focuses on problem areas and potentials for improvements in the collaboration based on win-win situations. The SWOT analysis results in action plans for the coming period. One year after the agreement with Wilson Logistics, Oticon has realised a substantial reduction in distribution costs. Although freight volume has increased by 13%, freight costs have been reduced by 9%.
www.oticon.com

Customer Relationship Management (CRM)

Customers, and therefore customer relations, are one of the company's most important assets. Logically, it is crucial for companies to consider the best manner to care for and service their customers. As a result, it is no longer sufficient for most companies to focus solely on the continuous sales process in relation to customers. Instead, there is a tendency to create a strategy for each chosen relationship in order to lead these interactions in a goal-oriented manner towards the company's overall strategy process and supply chain strategy.

Precisely the words chosen: relationships, or strategic relationships, are worth noting, as entering into closer relationships with customers is both demanding in terms of resources and connected with increased relationship costs from the supplier's perspective. Closer relations and integration will, in this way, demand increased resources from sales and management, and it will be necessary to earmark resources for the integration of processes; tailoring logistics, service, and administration, according to the customer's needs. Most investments made during this stage are irreversible. Therefore, the customers chosen for close integration and long-lasting cooperation should be carefully evaluated in relation to the company's strategic focus.

The vendor will often experience that there are several customers interested in entering into close forms of cooperation in order to attain as many benefits as possible from the relationship. This situation can be difficult for the supplier if there is no reciprocal interest in close cooperation. Therefore, it can be beneficial for vendor companies to act proactively, based on an analysis of the company's supply chain network, and categorise which customers are most desirable for which types of relationships. They may also assess which processes can be managed at the lowest possible cost.

CRM as a concept

The phrase: "the customer is in the centre," has been said and written so many times that its meaning is almost completely watered down. The customer is also in focus in the definition of the SCM concept. But who is the customer? How can the customer be held onto for the longest possible period? How do the company ensure that its business processes harmonise with the customer's expectations? And how can the resources available best be used for "customer care" and development of customer relations?

These are some of the questions that the CRM concept contributes to answering through its methods and tools. With CRM, the marketing focus that companies have directed towards the market and the customer, including customer relations, integration between business processes, systems, and organisations, can be broadened and developed. The focus today is much more oriented towards long-lasting relationships, increased information exchange, and consolidation of knowledge about a given customer, in order to create increased value for both the customer and the supplier companies. The win-win philosophy is thus also intrinsic to the CRM concept.

CRM is a business strategy – an attitude towards employees and customers – that rests on a number of processes and systems. The goal is to construct long-term relationships, and thereby add

87

value for the customer and the company through understanding of individual needs and preferences.[9]

CRM is about more than just marketing; it is to a high degree a management concept and a system for managing and controlling customer relations.

The point is creating a CRM *strategy* in relation to the company's customers, to clarify which markets/customers, products/services, and sales channels/processes, should be included in the company's future relationship control focus. And what face does the company want to meet its customers with in the future?

A robust CRM strategy is an important foundation for operationalising the overall SCM strategy, as the CRM strategy creates guidelines and priorities in relation to the customer, business processes, the organisation, and choice of IT system.

In connection with the drawing up of a CRM strategy, a certain correlation with the SCM component model (Chapter 2) can be observed. The SCM component model chooses also to focus on the strategic selection of cooperative partners, which are to be involved in the SCM network structure; the processes that are to be coupled to different relationships, as well as the level of integration that is to be incorporated in the individual relationships. In addition to these similarities, a portion of the CRM concept and thereby the CRM strategy focuses on how the internal customer management process can be improved upon.

Completing a CRM strategy will often take quite a while, as a thorough analysis of the selected/non-selected companies and an evaluation of the consequences of choosing/not choosing them is necessary in order to ensure a reasonable implementation of the concept. The only way of ensuring that long-term relationships are entered into with the most profitable and strategically important customers, is to down-prioritise or completely reject customers who do not fit into the category of profitability and strategic relevance. This process will most certainly lead to heated discussions among sales managers.

Also, discussions will almost always arise internally in sales departments regarding how closely the relationship and thereby the integration of different business processes should be in relation to different customers, not to mention which services should be provided.

---

[9] CRM håndbogen (2001)

Here, the goal of a CRM strategy is to construct a bond between the customers chosen and the company's other processes, for example: planning, production, and purchasing, which will enable the production flow to be optimised.

Besides addressing the issue of which customers should be included in or excluded from the integration process and choosing the level of cooperation, CRM is also about creating a joint internal process for customer management for different groups of customers.

The implementation of the CRM concept involves breaking down internal customer-focused departments and expressing the need for making the necessary organisational changes, so that the organisation can support new tasks. It is a good idea to spend time on explaining the changes and the motivation behind their implementation through a well-prepared change management plan, so that internal opposition can be eliminated as early on as possible.[10]

Another important task in connection with the implementation of the CRM strategy is contact to and involvement of the customer. Choosing a customer for a potential long-term relationship is the first step. The next step is finding out if the customer also expresses interest in such a relationship. The CRM concept's customer approach will always offer a better customer service, but in order to achieve the benefits of a close cooperation with the customer, it is necessary to design a plan for how the future integration can be developed so that both parties benefit.[11]

The characteristics of a company's customer relationships are not the outcome of unilateral 'sales' activity by the seller. Instead, they are the result of the combined actions and intentions of both supplier and customer, and of other companies elsewhere in the network that surrounds them.[12]

The CRM concept can in principle be divided into two parts: an overall analysis of the company's customer base according to the principles in the portfolio model,[13] and an internal optimising of the customer management process, including information management, service, order administration, and sales channels. The latter of these two parts is primarily related to a reduction of transaction costs in connection

---

[10] See also the section on "Function or Process Orientation" in this chapter for a further discussion of process orientation.
[11] Chapter 6 illustrates how CRM affects creation of value in the supply chain.
[12] Ford et al., 1997
[13] See Chapter 2

with management of the individual customer, plus the development of a foundation that allows the company's customers to receive the highest level of service possible.

The car industry is a good example. Previously, cars were sold by manufacturers through dealers with as much extra equipment as possible; in other words, a push sale. Today, a slow change towards a pull sale can be observed, in that customers can tailor-make their own car on the Internet. The order from the customer goes directly to the car manufacturer and the selected dealer.

In this way, CRM suddenly becomes not only about better customer relations, but also about re-thinking the supply chain from product information, to sales and ordering, and further on to production and distribution. The goal is to adjust the company's business processes so that both the customers' expectations and the company's business needs are met.

The CRM concept exists both as a theoretical perspective, emphasising primarily the choosing of relationships, and as a software solution supporting the management of customer relations and sales channels.

IT solutions/tools that support CRM

The amount of information available to people in their everyday lives is greater than ever, both privately and professionally. Paradoxically, this massive supply of information has resulted in customers having ever-greater expectations of a company's ability to maintain perspective, while at the same time, more and more companies lose their ability to maintain perspective. It is precisely perspective that is the determining factor when companies change from a transaction-focused to a more relation-oriented point of view. As a result, the ability to survey customer relations across the borders of the total business processes is a key factor.

It should be possible to incorporate all of the information the company receives from the customer in the complete picture of the customer, which is automatically generated. It is impossible to manage this process through manual work processes in most companies. As a result, it is frequently necessary to consider implementing an IT system that can manage integration and consolidation of customer information. The intention is that all employees who have customer contact can access this information.

For many years now, companies have focused on getting their ERP (Enterprise Resource Planning) solutions in place so that BI (Business Intelligence) historic data connected to customer related transactions can be accessed. How much have we sold? How much have we earned? Have we delivered on time? This process and the ability to answer these types of questions is the first step towards understanding the customer better.

With CRM as the software solution, the information platform can be expanded to include a number of functions that support the customer management process. Examples of these functions are described in the following sections.

Sales Force Automation

One area of specification could be that seller-documented inquiries, leads, opportunities, order activity, and meetings, are collected in a single sales tool, which the seller has as a supporting tool in connection with customer visits.

The seller could additionally achieve better planning of customer meetings, be on the cutting edge with the customer's history and needs prior to meetings, and be able to process transactions directly, during the visit to the customer.

Sales Force Automation gives companies a platform on which to document the sellers' knowledge for use in the implementation of uniform sales processes.

Call Centre

More and more companies have begun using a call centre to serve customers and other in-coming calls. This type of service department can document complaints, potential demand or requests, customer activity, and the status of customer issues.

"Call Centre" is used as a general title for an integrated point of contact for the customer. All transactions that are directly related to a customer can be integrated in a call centre, which allows the employee to see all of the customer's activities, as well as process the largest portion of customer related transactions. A call centre can be integrated through CTI (Computer Telephone Integration), which means that both in-coming and out-going calls can be handled. This integration process allows, for example, a customer to be identified by their telephone number, and their information to be accessible when their call is received.

Most CTI systems can also manage e-mail, fax, and, as a new feature, VoiceOver IP and CoBrowsing.

The call centre often has 'scripts,' which allow the employee to ensure the customer a uniform or homogenous experience, while also ensuring that all relevant questions are asked and the answers documented.

Internet

The Internet has become a new channel for sales and customer service. However, not all products and services can be sold equally well over the Internet. However, for products that are sold through frequent transactions, great savings in transactions costs can be achieved by selling over the Internet.

Most CRM systems can manage areas where there are often large transactions over the Internet. These may include enquiries surrounding the processing of orders, order status, product information, and changing of customer information. These costs can be included under relationship costs.

Marketing

With help from the information platform, it is possible for the company to achieve a more goal-oriented approach to customers. Based on the accessible customer information, target groups can be identified and focused on through more direct contact or an advertising campaign.

Key Account Management (KAM)

The goal of the KAM structure is to give more focused attention to strategic customers. By having an information platform based on ERP and CRM solutions, where customer data can be collected and analysed with Business Intelligence (BI), the company's contact person or people have an excellent opportunity to be well informed about a company's situation in relation to an individual strategic customer.

Business Intelligence (BI)

It is impossible to have a well-functioning CRM system without BI. This reality is based on the fact that the information, and thereby the key to understanding the customer's needs, is often spread over several systems. With BI, a report structure can be established that allows for the measurement and evaluation of the customer's present situation. Likewise, the customer's future needs can be analysed and estimated. Costs can be planned and simulated, and finally, the process can be optimised and executed based on the measured results.

Integration with the customer

The SCM concept has encouraged focus on the optimisation of the supply chain through the integration of the customers' and the suppliers' processes, especially in cases where there have been many transactions between them. Previously, integration was primarily achieved through EDI solutions.

Recently, other IT solutions have appeared on the market that supports this process. Communication platforms (portals) allow selected customers to make relevant transactions connected to the company's internal processes directly, through either front end or back office systems. This possibility has been predicted to be one of the greatest areas of improvement within sales processes and thereby customer relations. Figure 4.4 illustrates the CRM concept's link to the company's IT platform.

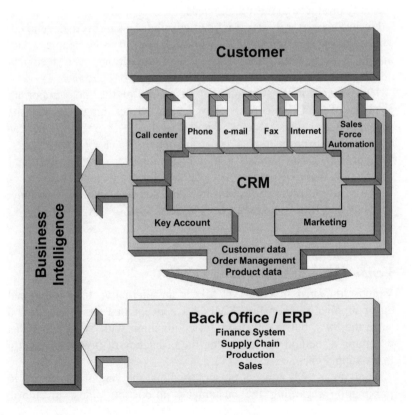

Figure 4.4 CRM-model

The CRM concept's system functions are placed in the front end while being integrated in the back office, which is the company's internal control system. All data is stored in a shared data warehouse. By integrating with the company's back office, and thereby their order system, production planning, and distribution, the supplier is well on its way to realising a pull sales strategy in relation to the customer. Louis Poulsen Lighting is one of the Danish companies that have had success with this type of project.

Louis Poulsen Lighting (LPL)[14] has used several CRM components to improve their relationship to their customers. First and foremost, they have changed their product range in order to meet customers' needs for tailor-made lamp solutions. LPL has implemented a product configuration that makes it possible for customers to order lamps specially produced to meet their needs.

Furthermore, a self-service Internet solution has been developed. This solution gives customers, employees, and data companies more insight into product information, light calculations, and technical documentation for the combination the customer has chosen.

The integration of solutions has been one of the most important elements of the CRM concept. This area is further integrated with the production and sales systems. Parallel to the CRM project, LPL has optimised their production in order to support the new CRM strategy. The goal of the new strategy is to reduce inventory, optimise customer satisfaction, and to develop a new platform for product information.

The solution has already been implemented in Denmark, Germany, England, and U.S.A., and will be introduced to all of LPL's subsidiaries in future.

Vendor Managed Inventory (VMI)

Vendor Managed Inventory (VMI) is an alternative to a traditional buyer/supplier relationship. VMI is a concept that has been around since the 80's, but is only now, in conjunction with SCM and ECR, becoming a method for increasing the efficiency of inventory control in the supply chain.

Applying a VMI concept presupposes that the vendor has access to information regarding the customer's production plans, inventory,

---

[14] Louis Poulsen is a Lighting company founded in 1874. Turnover 270 Mill. Euro and 1100 employees. www.louispoulsen.com

ordering, and sales forecasts. After this stage of openness is achieved, it becomes the responsibility of the supplier to manage and replenish the customer's inventory. The parties agree on more precise guidelines for minimum and maximum inventory levels, as well as for when ownership is transferred and payments are made.

The information exchange between parties can occur through a traditional EDI transfer of information, or be facilitated by exchanging XML files over the Internet. The advantage for the vendor is that it can organise its production planning and material supply far in advance and thereby utilise its capacity more efficiently and with a more stable workload. For the customer company, the primary benefit is that administration of purchasing can be relieved of a number of routine acts, goods receiving control, as well as a reduction of the risk of running out of inventory. The work hours thus released can instead be focused on the development of strategic alliances and the purchasing of critical goods.

In comparison to a traditional customer/supplier form of cooperation, VMI offers the opportunity of eliminating duplicate functions between vendor and customer, delays in deliveries, out-of-date merchandise etc. At the same time, VMI gives the supplier the chance to optimise its internal capacity utilisation and material flow.

Oticon, a market manager in the hearing aid industry, has approximately 250 active suppliers, of which 20 suppliers account for 70% of the purchasing volume. These 20 suppliers are furthermore classified into:

1. Trivial suppliers
2. Critical suppliers
3. Non-critical suppliers

There are 15 critical suppliers, supplying, for example, integrated circuits, EMC, customised components, and unique components. Oticon engages in close cooperation and partnership with these suppliers because they usually handle designs that are unique to Oticon. Several of them are sole source suppliers. An example is the collaboration between William Demant and the U.S.-based Starkey regarding a small FM receiver to be clicked onto hearing aids to improve hearing, which must be compatible with FM compatible microphones installed at some sites, such as conference rooms.

Manufacturing of hearing aids is a niche area. Oticon is a small customer for some of the large electronic manufacturers of electronic components. Oticon requests a minimum of one month of stock from its suppliers, depending on the agreement made with the supplier. Oticon has had more than 10 years (up to 30 years) of close cooperation with a handful of suppliers.

Oticon prefers not to engage in single sourcing (there are, for example, two suppliers of transducers). In order to ensure availability of components, it maintains contact with all suppliers of hearing aid components. Oticon has high production volume with high dependence on process.

Oticon has implemented Vendor Managed Inventory (VMI) in order to help its critical suppliers with their forecasting and production planning. With VMI, suppliers get automatic notification when the inventory level falls below a certain amount, which is based on weekly usage information and production consumption over 10 days. Currently, there are about 12 suppliers using VMI. Oticon teaches its suppliers about the benefits of VMI (for example, for production planning and for preventing the bullwhip effect), although it has encountered some resistance from the suppliers.

Oticon receives a financial report from the suppliers, and the finance department performs a risk analysis of the suppliers. There are several internal auditors that are responsible for supplier qualification, which can take three months, and sometimes even longer. The qualification involves quality inspection as well as inspection by technical experts. Oticon's key suppliers are also audited once a year.

Efficient Consumer Response (ECR)

In the beginning of the 90's, the first initiatives towards greater efficiency in the retail supply chain surfaced. Efficient Consumer Response (ECR) focused on cooperation between the retail link and retail vendors. A closer cooperation between these parties should create the possibility of direct customer response throughout the supply chain. The goal was to increase efficiency in the flow of goods and to utilise the data the retail stores' electronic cash registers collected.

"This new reality required a fundamental reconsideration of the most effective way of delivering the right products to consumers, at the right price. Non-standardised operational practices, and

the rigid separation of the traditional roles of manufacturer and retailer threatened to block the supply chain unnecessarily, and failed to exploit the synergies that came from powerful new information technologies, and planning tools"[15]

The ECR concept focuses on four branch specific core areas:
- Efficient store assortment (category management)
- Efficient replenishment
- Efficient promotion (sales campaigns)
- Efficient product introduction

The core area for which the greatest potential for savings was identified was connected with optimising delivery to retailers, i.e. inventory management and replenishment. These were also the areas that were later focused on during the application and implementation of the ECR concept. ECR builds upon already existing concepts such as VMI and Quick Response Systems.

ECR in Arla Foods

In the mid-90's Arla Foods[16] established an ECR (Efficient Consumer Response) cooperative agreement with an English retail chain. The goal of this cooperation is to ensure a maximum delivery time of 24 hours, counted from when the order is received to delivery. Arla Foods has developed an advance inventory in England in order to achieve this delivery target. The individual stores give daily orders for Arla Foods products. These orders are gathered from all stores covered by the retail chain's regional distribution centre. Arla Foods receives the entire order from the distribution centre and delivers within 24 hours to the relevant distribution centre, which in turn is responsible for delivery to the individual stores.

Savings in inventory and handling costs are the advantages for the customer. Arla Foods enjoys more precise information concerning actual sales in the stores and can thereby reduce their risk for out of stock situations, or expired products resulting from the customer

---

[15] ECR.com, 2002

[16] Arla Foods is a Cooperative owned by approx. 7,200 Swedish and 8,300 Danish milk producers with an annual turnover of 5,1 billion Euro. In December 2004 Arla Foods and the Dutch dairy company Campina merged into Campina Arla, now the largest dairy company in Europe. www.arlafoods.com

company having too large inventories. Today, the cooperative relationship with the English retail chain is actually closer to the principles of the CPFR concept. The term ECR is becoming outdated and the balance of power is almost completely in the retail chain's favour. These factors make "masked cooperation models" unnecessary. CPFR is also a cooperation model, but is controlled to a much greater extent through a cooperative method, which plots a directional course that the vendor can follow.

Source: Aksel Poulstrup, Logistics Manager, Arla Foods 2002

Collaborative Planning, Forecasting and Replenishment (CPFR)

In 1995 Collaborative Planning, Forecasting & Replenishment (CPFR) was introduced in connection with a pilot project involving Wal-Mart, Warner-Lambert, Benchmarking Partners, SAP and Manugistics. Based on these experiences, the Voluntary Inter-industry Commerce Standards (VICS) introduced a guideline in 1998 for CPFR collaboration. Whereas previous methods such as VMI (vendor-managed inventory) or CRP (continuous replenishment programme) mainly focused on collaboration concerning replenishment/reordering, the CPFR concept also promotes integration of planning and forecasting processes.

VICS defines CPFR as "a collection of new business practices that leverage the Internet and electronic data interchange in order to radically reduce inventories and costs while improving customer service". This definition suggests that the Internet and electronic data interchange (EDI) are substantial prerequisites for CPFR. Other definitions, such as the one made by ECR Europe (2001) are more general and refer to collaboration rather than EDI: "CPFR is a cross-industry initiative designed to improve the supplier/manufacturer/ retailer relationship through co-managed planning processes and shared information". In spite of the minor discrepancies in the definitions of CPFR, there is little doubt that the ruling perception of CPFR is based on the VICS definition.

The CPFR process builds to a large extent on the exchange of information among collaboration partners. This exchange of information can be carried out through the use of various technologies such as EDI (Electronic Data Interchange), private networks or the Internet (XML). For the processing of information a large number of software programmes have been developed to support the CPFR processes (e.g. Manugistics; i2 Technologies, Numetrix, SAP APO, Oracle, Baan and PeopleSoft). For the sake of simplicity and in order to create an overview we have chosen to structure the generic VICS business model by dividing it into a planning phase (Steps 1-2), a forecasting phase (Steps 3-8) and a replenishment phase (Step 9). Taken as a whole, these steps can be seen as a cyclic and iterative approach to achieving consensus on supply chain forecasts, see Table 4.1 below.

Step	Activity	Description
1	Develop Front-End Agreement	A front-end agreement is developed. Criteria for success are established. Identification of the CPFR project owners in the companies. Financial reward and contribution system is agreed upon.
2	Create Joint Business Plan	A joint business plan for the areas of collaboration is created. Plans regarding advertising campaigns etc are made.
3-5	Sales Forecast Collaboration	The parties get together and use their individual customer demand prognoses to establish a common prognosis. In case of deviation from the forecast, the partners meet to discuss deviations and to update the common forecast.
6-8	Order Forecast Collaboration	The partners share replenishment plans and discuss deviations and constraints.
9	Order Generation	The reordering process/goods flow is initiated. Result data is discussed (POS, orders, shipments) Forecast deviation and stock level problems are identified and solved.

Table 4.1 An overview of CPFR activities.

An important issue for CPFR is that the successful application of the concept consists of more than partners who are merely opening up and exchanging information. The predominant part of the process consists of partners joining in a number of joint planning activities. That is why some authors see CPFR as an evolution of Efficient Consumer

Response (ECR), vendor managed inventory systems (VMI) and continuous replenishment programmes (CRP). The essence of CPFR can be characterised as addressing the deficiencies found in those previous forms of collaborative arrangements, such as:

- The influence of promotions in the creation of the sales forecast (and its influence on inventory management policy)
- The influence of changing demand patterns in the creation of the sales forecast (and its influence on inventory management policy)
- The common practice of holding inventory levels high to guarantee product availability on the shelves;
- The lack of general synchronisation (or co-ordination) in the manufacturer's functional departments (sales/commercial, distribution and production planning);
- The multiple forecasting developed within the same company (marketing, financing, purchasing and logistics).

Different levels of CPFR

In its conceptual origin, CPFR is relatively comprehensive considering the amount of processes and relations involved. Therefore, CPFR can with advantage be divided into three levels depending on the integration and extent of the collaboration. [17] In figure 4.5 the scope of collaboration is shown on the y-axis indicating the number of business processes in the collaboration. The x-axis shows the depth of collaboration measuring the integration of the processes in the collaboration.

---

[17] Based on Skjøtt-Larsen et al (2003a)

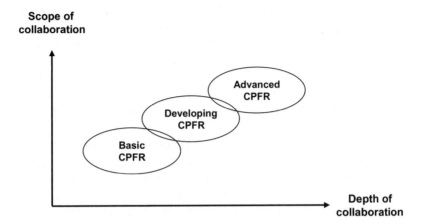

Figure 4.5 Different levels of CPFR

Basic CPFR

Basic CPFR collaboration only involves few business processes and a limited integration with trading partners. The supply chain actors who have adopted this approach to CPFR will usually choose a few key processes relevant to precisely their form of collaboration with customers or suppliers. An example might be a supplier who enters into a collaborative relation with a retailer based on exchange of stock level data. The data are used in connection with the respective partners' order planning. The collaboration comprises one single business process – order planning – but the parties neither co-ordinate nor synchronise the process. Therefore, the collaborative relationship reflects a low degree of integration. Frequently, this form of collaboration is the starting point of all collaborative initiatives.

The reason why a firm enters into basic CPFR-collaboration is the advantage of increased information exchange, minimising the costs of transactions. However, from a theoretical perspective, it is the trade-off between the benefits from close collaboration with chosen partners and the drawbacks from being tied to certain partners that decides whether a firm will proceed with increased integration. Thus, the supply chain actors who participate in basic CPFR-collaboration have a transaction cost approach to collaboration.

Developed CPFR

Compared to the basic CPFR model, developed CPFR-collaboration is characterised by increased integration in several collaboration areas.

When the collaborative parties start to co-ordinate data and information exchange by making agreements about what type of information to exchange and how they should respond to the exchanged data, integration is increasing. Two supply chain actors who establish an exchange of stock level and forecast data might illustrate developed CPFR. Increased integration in collaboration might e.g. be to hand over the responsibility for replenishment to the supplier.

The incentive to enter into this type of collaboration is primarily based on a wish to make delivery faster and more precise, which is more feasible with a frequent exchange of information. The motive in basic CPFR was very focused on costs, whereas the approach of developed CPFR is more focused on improving client services as a way to increase trade. However, cost considerations still play a role, as more accurate forecast figures will improve the use of capacity and stock keeping. Thus, the supply chain actors, who enter into developed CPFR-collaboration, have a network approach, focusing primarily on frequent exchange of information and generation of trust in the relationships.

Advanced CPFR

An advanced CPFR-model differs from developed CPFR by taking collaboration a little further than mere data exchange. In addition to the exchange of data, collaboration deals with synchronising the dialogue between the parties. The collaboration has been expanded to co-ordinate processes within forecasting, replenishment and planning. The planning processes may be additionally decomposed to involve collaboration on production planning, product development, transport planning and marketing activities. At frequent meetings, all relevant business processes are co-ordinated on the basis of a joint objective. The joint objective usually focuses on developing a certain group of products, even though the respective parties may have different goals. As long as their goals are somewhat complementary, e.g. if they have a certain connection that makes it easier to achieve the respective goals through closer collaboration, there is a good basis for CPFR-like collaboration. In an ordinary producer–retailer relationship, the producer will enter into collaboration on forecasting and replenishment to improve production planning and reduce stock levels, which in turn should reduce the running costs. The retailer's goal, on the other hand, is to have the right goods in the right place at the right time to increase sales. In other words, CPFR-collaboration may fulfil completely different goals.

Apart from improving planning, which will lead to increased sales and minimized costs in the supply chain, the motive for entering advanced CPFR-collaboration also includes a wish to develop qualifications to continue improvement of the company's processes. Such a learning process leads to a more agile and changeable supply chain which is why it tends to be more competitive than rival in nature. Supply chain actors who enter into this type of collaboration have a fundamental network-theoretical approach to collaboration. However, the approach is combined with a resource-based perspective/competency perspective that emphasizes development of competencies and learning between firms.

Based on the discussion above, the central differences in the contents of the three forms of CPFR are illustrated in table 4.2.

Dimension	Basic CPFR	Developed CPFR	Advanced CPFR
Shared information	Sales orders and confirmation Inventory data	Demand data Order planning data Promotion data Production data	Demand data Order planning data Promotion data Production data
Degree of discussion	No	Some	Frequently
Co-ordination/ synchronisation	No	Some	All activities
Competence development	No	No	Knowledge
Evaluation	No	No	Experiences
Type of relationship	Transactional	Information sharing	Mutual learning
Theoretical explanation	TCA	Network	Resource- and competence-based

Table 4.2 Dimensions of the different levels of CPFR

Efficient Governance Structures

All three levels of CPFR collaboration start with transaction costs determined through negotiating with other independent firms. Transaction costs are not only related to buying and selling goods, they may just as well be related to information exchange and payment flows, where information exchange is a central part of the CPFR-collaboration. Transaction costs can be divided into costs from establishing contact with the new trade partner (searching costs), costs from working out a new contract with the partner (bargaining costs) and costs related to monitoring the partner's fulfilment of the contract (control costs).

The level of the costs depends on three characteristics related to the transactions: the level of uncertainty under which the transaction is carried out, the frequency of the transactions and the degree of asset specificity (Williamson, 1985). The transaction cost theory implies the risk of opportunistic behaviour. Based on the assumption that there will always be some uncertainty in a relationship, it is possible to place the three forms of CPFR in the framework shown in figure 4.6 determined by the dimensions frequency and degree of asset specific investments.

	Investment characteristics		
Frequency	Non-specific	Mixed	Idiosyncratic
Occasional	*Market governance (classic contract)*	*Trilateral governance (neoclassic contract)*	
Recurrent	*Market governance* **Basic CPFR**	*Bilateral governance* **Developed CPFR**	*Unified governance* **Advanced CPFR**

Figure 4.6 Governance structures and transaction characteristics of different levels of CPFR

The reason why the parties want to develop a closer form of collaboration is the high frequency of transactions between the parties. Therefore, the differences between the CPFR forms must be found by looking at the bottom part of the framework above focusing on the investment characteristics. The investment in idiosyncratic assets between the collaboration partners functions as a safeguard ensuring that none of the partners will act in an opportunistic way. In a basic CPFR-relation, the investments are not very specific and might often be applied to other relations. The investments may be simple technical data exchanging programmes that are only geared to deal with a limited amount of data. In relation to Williamson's governance structure, basic CPFR will be managed through market regulations (or classical contract).

However, in developed and advanced CPFR, the investments for both parties will be greater owing to the high level of information

104

exchange. We distinguish between 'hard investments' and 'soft investments'. By hard investments, we mean investments in material resources that can only be applied to one CPFR-relation, e.g. technical investments such as IT-software to carry out a specific CPFR-collaboration. However, soft investments in human resources are very important when implementing CPFR. The employees must have the necessary knowledge enabling them to handle the new IT-based processes of data exchange within planning, forecasting and replenishment. In a similar way, it may be necessary to invest in good social relations between the parties. The more complex developed CPFR will be based on a bilateral governance structure and advanced CPFR will be approaching a unified structure. According to this division, we might say that a safeguard against opportunistic behaviour in the simple form of CPFR collaboration may be part of a traditional legal contract. However, developed and advanced CPFR implies that the parties are fairly integrated. Moreover, it is assumed that a joint spirit of collaboration exists, which will keep the parties from acting opportunistic. That is why it is only necessary to work out relational contracts, where the spirit behind the contract is more important than the terms of the contract itself. An alternative safeguard in relation to contracts is private agreements, where the parties can enter into joint ventures or make symmetric investments in the relationship (credible commitments). In some cases, this form of regulation may be more relevant than contracts in CPFR collaboration, where the relationship is constantly developing and regularly taking on new shapes making it difficult to specify the terms of relationship in a contract.

CPFR and SCM

There is a certain similarity in method when one compares the CPFR committee's[18] and the Global Supply Chain Forum's (GSCF)[19] suggestions and criteria for entering into partnerships. The CPFR method is distinct from the SCM concept in that it specifies to a much greater degree how the integration, and hence cooperation, with regard to the chosen processes should be implemented. At the same time, the CPFR concept makes use of the possibilities that the Internet presents, in particular in relation to the integration between the parties involved.

---

[18] Examples of companies involved in the CPFR forum are Wal-Mart, Target, Procter & Gamble, Kodak, Heineken, HP, and SAP.
[19] Global Supply Chain Forum consists of a number of large companies that work with methods of implementing SCM.

The main difference between SCM and CPFR is that CPFR focuses on the entire process and planning activities between the involved companies. SCM grows from an overall management perspective of the supply chain, which focuses on the choice of the supply chain's strategic composition, as well as the development of relationships between the cooperative partners.

CPFR focuses on all three processes of collaboration: planning, forecasting, and replenishment, all of which support the four main categories earlier identified in relation to ECR. The SCM concept conceptualises in broader terms which processes can be integrated between companies. However, the SCM concept does not go to the same depths in its suggestions for how integration of processes can take place. One can argue that the process the company's management goes through in connection with the SCM concept, for example, choosing the central relationships in the network, selecting the processes that are to be integrated with the chosen cooperation partners, and deciding the level of closeness of integration, are presupposed for the implementation of the CPRF concept.

The CPFR committee was clearly inspired by ECR and the thinking behind SCM when they undertook the continued development of ECR as a tool for the everyday necessities market. This inspiration can, for example, be seen in the focus on win-win and integration. CPFR distinguishes itself by its focus on the operationalisation of the integration process, as well as the inclusion of IT development possibilities that support optimisation and integration of the individual processes.

The fundamental thinking behind optimising the supply chain is in principle the same for both SCM and CPFR. In general, though, CPFR is more operational in its focus than the SCM concept, in that it starts with individual processes that it is relevant to integrate in cooperative agreements between retailers and finished product vendors.

5. Information Systems as a Lever for Company Processes

As integration in the supply chain is increased, so do complexity of information sharing and decision-making increase. Integrated planning systems can to great advantage be used to support information exchange and decision processes. These benefits arise from the ability to collect and deal with relevant information, which provides for a clear and rapid picture of the situation. [20]

Global competition means that customers' expectations are central to all company activities. The trend is to move from a push to a pull strategy. As much as possible of production and distribution is based on the customers' orders. As a result, customer requirements are to a large degree the controlling factors of the company's processes.

The customer also expects to be met by the same "face" regardless of place, time, or the reason for their enquiry. In order to be able to deliver this service and manage a pull strategy for the supply chain, it is necessary for the company to harmonise its processes throughout different product groups, divisions and countries.

ERP and APS – Integrated Planning Systems

Integrated administration systems, of which SAP R/3, Oracle, Baan, and Navision are the best-known in Europe, are referred to as ERP systems (Enterprise Resource Planning). ERP systems are standard systems in which all the sub processes in all the company's functions are integrated with each other and thereby affect each other. For example, when a warehouse employee enters a goods delivery into the system, the transaction is simultaneously registered in the warehouse system, which is evaluated by the accounting department. The transaction is also registered in a quantitative manner, so that the materials buyer who is responsible for purchasing the goods also has the opportunity to follow replenishment levels. ERP systems are

---

[20] Most of chapter 5 is written by business process manager Camilla Fink, Corporate Supply Chain, Carlsberg A/S.

focused on internal optimising of the company, which is the first step towards optimising the entire supply chain.

In recent years more advanced planning systems have arrived on the market: APS systems, which can further optimise processes. This optimisation occurs through integrating and sharing information between business partners in the supply chain, as well as by including this information in planning. Above and beyond this procedure APS systems are equipped with mathematically algorithms, which are capable of handling multiple capacity limitations from several different companies.

The Industry Perspective

IT systems comprise a wide variety of functions that can support and optimise the supply chain's processes. The areas that it can be beneficial for a given company to concentrate on are determined by the industry the company is a part of. As mentioned in the introduction to this chapter, the demands placed on a company's processes are derived from the customer's expectations. As industries operate based on largely differing markets with different customers, process characteristics vary correspondingly.

Table 5.1 indicates which processes, in different industries, can be improved in the supply chain through IT systems.

H: Highly advisable M: Somewhat advisable L: Unnecassary Processes	Consumer Goods / Commodoties	Consumer Goods / High Tech	Energy	Medical & Pharmaceuticals	Food / Provisions	Other Industries
Forecasting	H	H	M	M	H	H
Sales and Operations Planning	H	H	H	M	H	M
Supply Planning	M	H	M	M	H	M
Rough Planning of Production	M	H	H	M	H	M
Order Processing	H	H	M	H	H	M
Customer Service	H	H	M	L	M	M
Distribution and Transport	M	H	L	L	H	L
Detail Production Planning	L	M	L	L	L	M
Product Development	H	H	L	H	M	H

Table 5.1 Processes, which can be improved by IT systems.

Table 5.1 shows that, for example, the transport planning process varies from industry to industry. Within the food/provisions industry there is a tendency for the producer to be responsible for transportation from the factory to the distribution centre and the retailer (customer). This tendency can be observed because food products often require special care and handling during transport. The consumer goods industry differs in this respect as a third party logistics company typically transports goods. The energy industry does not involve transport, as energy is typically distributed through wires (electricity) and pipes (distance heating).

Generally, table 5.1 shows that especially the consumer goods and food/provisions industries can benefit from implementing ERP and APS. After these industries come medical and pharmaceutical, and finally the energy and industrial sectors. This order approximately parallels the sequence of industries in which ERP and APS have gained footing.

Optimising Individual Processes

A producer of consumer goods will often have an internal supply chain composed of 3-4 stages, from factory to market. The industry is quite advanced in terms of optimising processes in the supply chain with ERP and APS, as a producer can attain great benefits simply by focusing on their internal supply chain. This type of company has an extensive internal distribution network, with intermediate inventories, which is quite in contrast to, for example, electricity networks. Consequently, the integration with both the customer and the supplier is developed and supported through IT systems.[21] Figure 5.1. shows a typical supply chain for a global producer of consumer goods.

---

[21] This situation can, for example, be observed in connection with the use of ECR and CPFR concepts, as discussed in Chapter 4.

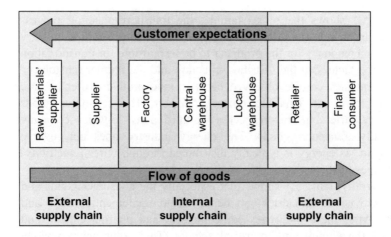

Figure 5.1 Transformation of customer's expectations in a supply chain.

All links in the consumer goods company's internal supply chain can act as both customer and supplier. As a result, the final customer's expectations apply as process requirements throughout the chain's links right back to the raw materials' supplier. In figure 5.1, the company's customer is the retailer and not the final consumer. The demands a retailer makes on a company will be directly derived from the expectations the final customer imposes upon the retailer.

Typical consumer expectations include the existence of a wide variety of producers, price categories, and levels of quality. The possibility of choosing between different varieties is attractive to consumers, who obviously want the product that is best suited to their needs. The customer should be able to take the product from the shelf and go directly home with it; therefore, products with long delivery times will often be eliminated. The demands the consumer makes on the retailer require that the other links in the supply chain increase their focus on selected processes. In the following sections, the processes and the characteristics that are typical in relation to the supply chain will be examined from the producer's perspective. These areas include: forecasting, operational planning, supply planning, rough production planning, order management, distribution, and transport. For each process, the characteristics that result from the customer's expectations, as well as how the individual processes can be initially supported by ERP, and afterwards supported by APS planning, will be explained.

Forecasting

A forecast is an expression of the company's expected volume and value of sales, and is the basis for all material planning in the company. The forecast is involved in long-term operational planning, but is also adjusted and used in short-term supply planning and rough production planning, which operate with shorter timelines than operational planning.

The customer's expectation of being able to choose between different varieties of a product leads consumer goods companies to generate an increased amount of finished products. The products are characterised by a relatively short life cycle (6-12 months), meaning that last year's sales cannot necessarily be used to create a new relevant forecast. Marketing and frequent campaigns are utilised to maintain and increase market shares. As a result, historic sales figures are also influenced by these campaigns. Salespeople are typically given bonuses based on sales, which can sometimes cause seasonal fluctuations in sales resulting from salespeople trying to meet their budgets. The forecast generated for each market (country or region) is not limited to specific products, but focuses instead on what is sold from local inventories.

For the largest customer among the retail stores, it is normal that a common forecast is generated for future purchasing. Staff in charge of the local warehouses/inventories prepares a proposal, which is adjusted by the retailer before it is integrated in the overall forecast for the local market.

ERP can help create a forecast for products in groups, so that instead of just having a forecast for individual items, a broader prospective can be developed. Historic sales are automatically accessible in the system, based on sales orders, which have been keyed in and delivered earlier. The system itself can generate mathematic models, which best apply to the historical data, as well as produce a forecast based on the generated model. For new products, the forecast can be based on the sales history for the "old" product, which is being replaced, in order to avoid the problem of non-existing historic sales figures. When the forecast is released to planning, the system can automatically compare it with incoming sales orders, which replace the forecast with the incoming order quantities. It is thus ensured that the correct sales quantities are incorporated in planning, even though the entire forecast has been used.

APS systems have the same functionality as ERP, but are more flexible with regard to how the hierarchy of a forecast is structured, and how amounts are aggregated and disaggregated between levels. Another important factor is the standard functionality of eliminating campaign sales from the historic data, so that the data basis for new forecasts is adjusted accordingly.

In addition to an internal forecast calculation, it is possible to integrate the forecasting process with business partners, as an APS system allows for separate user interfaces for key customers, which can in turn be made accessible over the Internet. In this way, a forecast can be proposed and other relevant information can thus be made accessible to the customer. After the customer comments on this information, it is returned electronically to the producer. This process integrates the customer in the company's planning process and improves the quality of planning.

Operational Planning

Similarly to the forecasting process, operational planning has a number of characteristics that can be derived from the consumers' demands and expectations.

Consumer goods such as toys and vacation-related or weather-related products often have seasonal patterns. As a result, above and beyond the normal production planning, it is also necessary to follow the seasonal pattern throughout the year in order to ensure production capacity. As the production system typically consists of employees working for 8-hour working days, the capacity will typically be 8, 16, or 24 hours per day, determined by demand. Since it can take time to both mobilise and dismiss a working force, it is important to know well ahead of time how many employees are needed during different times of the year.

When future budgets are planned, it is also important to consider whether there is a lack of employees, or if the situation calls for the production capacity to be expanded. Sometimes advertising campaigns can be placed strategically, so that capacity demands are evened out. Transport capacities in terms of distribution, which are normally handled by a third party logistics supplier, do not enter into the equation.

In an integrated ERP system, data regarding the individual machine and shift capacities is already available. Based on the first generated forecast, the need for production capacity can be simulated, creating a basis for budget and strategic planning. Different business scenarios can also be simulated based on different forecasts.

APS systems integrate forecasting and budget organisation, and can be used to involve customers directly in operational planning. As a result, capacity limitations on the factory level can be included in planning, and can be applied on the market/customer level. Consequently, alternative warehousing levels can be adjusted to suit the needs of the markets/customers in good time. This possibility allows for the creation of a basis for a consensus forecast.

Supply Planning
The goal of supply chain planning can be briefly stated as planning that aims at meeting the consumer's needs in the best possible way given the supply and capacity possibilities available. The concrete tasks and challenges that characterise this process are, as mentioned in the introduction, dependent upon the consumer's demands and expectations.

The producing company typically has established a large network of markets through their local warehouses, factories, and sometimes a few central warehouses. Usually, there is a determined and preferred route from factory to market, in order to minimise transportation costs. Production demand for the individual products is calculated in reverse, based on the market's customer orders, forecast, safety supplies, and transportation time. Many raw materials within the high-tech industry have long delivery times, and it is therefore normal to engage in close cooperation with key vendors of critical components. This relationship ensures that delivery times are met, even on short notice.[22] Shared planning and vendor-managed inventories (VMI) are both aspects included in this type of relationship. Suppliers are chosen on the basis of continual evaluations in order to ensure that, for example, the quality, price, and delivery reliability agreed upon are maintained. As is the case in the purchasing of raw materials, the supply chain plan is used to adjust and purchase the necessary transport capacities.

If all the company's links in the internal supply chain use the same ERP system, it becomes possible to integrate planning in the different links. In this manner, demand can be transferred from local inventories to a centralised inventory (the next link), and possibly on to the factory. As ERP systems can only plan one location (market or factory) at a time, a planning sequence must be defined. The sequence guarantees that all markets have been planned and their input has been submitted to a central warehouse before plans are made for that

---

[22] This situation is exemplified in the B&O case.

location and the information is given to the factory, which is the last to be planned. If the markets do not have the same ERP system it can be difficult to establish the above-mentioned dependency order. The same situation results when factories deliver semi-manufactured goods to each other, as these create a loop in the sequence.

Purchasing, receiving, and invoice control are all ingredients in the planning system. Therefore, the information related to these activities is automatically collected for supplier evaluation. Different functions allow the construction of individual criteria and point systems, which can be aligned with data that already exists in the system, or which can be transferred automatically or manually.

In an APS system the sequence and planning of the entire network is self-defined in one stroke, regardless of which ERP system locality the information normally originates from. Unit lists from local campaigns are automatically broken down into the correct order, ensuring that all needs for all levels are planned correctly.

The optimal transportation route, from factory to local warehouses, can be calculated in the system by use of algorithms, which take costs and capacity limits into account. After this processing is completed, the result can be saved as the standard route. Safety inventories can be statistically determined, based on the history of uncertainty in both forecasting and delivery, hereby ensuring the optimal safety supplies corresponding to the desired level of customer service.

Some APS systems are able to automatically grant vendors access to long-term purchasing plans over the Internet, allowing for advance feedback on possible delivery problems. This same manner of cooperation is seen in relation to third-party suppliers, in regard to planning of transport capacities.

APS systems have very flexible functions in terms of making demand and inventory information available to vendors. This functionality allows suppliers to take on the responsibility for refilling specific components.

Rough Planning of Production

Production of, for example, high-tech consumer goods, will often include many levels in bill of materials (BOM). Semi-manufactured items are used in many varieties of finished goods and unit lists share production capacity. Because of the many dependencies between bill of materials, production planning can be exceedingly difficult to survey. Normally, the less strategic segments of production are outsourced to sub-suppliers, though the planning of production rests with the producer.

ERP systems can support a cross product structuring of the individual production machine groups. This ability simplifies planning and creates a basis for manual adjustments of capacity limits in production planning that are not standard in ERP.

APS systems can handle limitations from several BOM and machines, generating a physically feasible rough planning proposal. This possibility makes it unnecessary to examine the plan for each product/machine. Instead, the planner can concentrate on capacity issues. In cases where a sub-supplier is responsible for production, the plan, with the additional information necessary for cooperative adjustments, can be made available to the sub-supplier on the Internet. The sub-supplier is thus directly integrated in the company's rough planning process.

Distribution and Transport

Factories will typically send everything they produce to the closest central warehouse, as they rarely have large storage capacities. The central warehouse distributes the products to the market in response to demand. The products are pushed from the factory to the central warehouse, while they are pulled from the central warehouse to the market.

The central warehouse will often need to load the containers or trucks so that capacities are utilised to the fullest. As a result, a shipment will often be composed of many different products, which are distributed in cases of differing sizes. Sometimes the capacity is determined by volume, for example, coffee machines, and other times by weight, for example, batteries. The shipments from the factories are easy to pack, as whole pallets are sent, and trucks/containers are dispatched as soon as they are full. Most transport is outsourced to transport companies or forwarding agents, which limits the need for route optimising.

When supply is insufficient to meet the demand from all markets, the inventory is allocated among customers. If a market has planned a large campaign, with TV advertisements and special space allotments in stores, the product must be available. Therefore, it is important to know which markets take priority in conjunction with "internal backorders."

Since both ERP and APS systems are integrated with sales and inventory functions, the producer can see location specific information on sales orders, incoming deliveries, production orders for campaigns, and real-time warehouse inventory. This means that the producer can set up shipments when the local warehouse's inventory falls below the reordering level. If the central warehouse does not have sufficient supply to satisfy the demand from all the local warehouses, there is a logical foundation for determining which local warehouses have priority and when. These rules of priority can be used by the system to automatically generate the most appropriate shipment plan.

It is also possible, based on product characteristics, to generate "packing suggestions" for containers and trucks, in order to help utilise capacity. The shipment is sent electronically to the warehouse system, where the pull order and ramp ID are designated. Standard definitions and technology for sharing of shipping information enable the tracing of shipment status throughout the process, until the shipment is logged in as inventory at the destination. The recipient will normally receive information on the contents of the shipment, when it is sent. This information exchange will either occur through standard interfaces or via the Internet.

Order Management

The producer's order management process will be dictated by the need of retail stores for having a broad assortment available, and having all producers represented. When ordering it is standard procedure to check that the order line can be confirmed for a desired delivery date. If the product is not available through the local warehouse, in some cases an effort may be made to find an alternative warehouse. This decision is of course dependent upon the geographic possibilities within the internal supply chain.

If the warehouse does not have the desired product, one possibility is to substitute another product for a product variant that is back-ordered. As earlier mentioned, it is important that the products are available in the retail locations if there is currently a campaign/sale on the product. In this type of situation, the producer and customer may have agreed upon and confirmed the delivery of the involved products ahead of time, ensuring that the products can be delivered.

In an ERP system, in which the sales system is integrated with the inventory system, an order can be confirmed and the delivery date given when the customer keys in their order. When the order line is confirmed, the product will be reserved in the warehouse, and can no longer be used in another order. Sequences can be established to investigate the availability of a product in different inventories. As part of such a sequence, alternative products can be suggested based on whether or not the customer's data indicates interest in alternative suggestions.

Further, the functionality exists to establish maximum boundaries for the number of units an individual customer may purchase per period, thereby making advance reservations for particular customers. In cases of extremely high demand for particular products, this function can ensure customers who are running campaigns the amounts they have reserved. Sales orders from other customers will not be confirmed, even though the product is still in the inventory, as the units are reserved for another customer.

In the APS system it is possible to fine tune the search sequences and in the case of lacking inventory, search after available production capacity and raw material demand, in order to produce the product needed. After this search process is completed, the first available delivery date can be made available when orders are placed. If the proposed delivery date is accepted and the order line is confirmed, a production order to the factory will automatically be generated and the necessary raw materials will be reserved in the inventory.

Important Considerations in Connection with IT Implementation

The functions within ERP and APS systems now cover all traditional business arenas within a company, and are constantly updated. As described earlier, there is a rich possibility for optimising a company's supply chain processes and extending the chain electronically by integrating one's business partners in these processes. At the same time, it is necessary to emphasise that an IT system is not the same as optimising. There are just as many pitfalls as methods for avoiding them. This section will not provide a definitive method or examination of the topic, but instead go in depth with three fundamental dimensions.

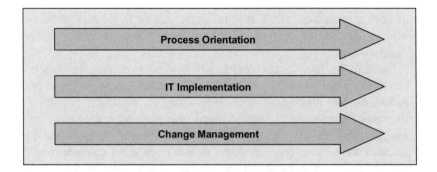

Figure 5.2 Dimensions in an optimisation project

As seen in Figure 5.2, an optimisation project should above and beyond the technical implementation of IT also include the dimensions of process orientation and change management. These dimensions are parallel in a project. Even though different people typically deal with the tasks in each dimension, it is important that there is close integration between these areas.

Process Orientation includes all the duties that are connected to the business processes. This dimension identifies and defines the optimising goals for the individual processes. At the same time, the processes must be able to ensure support of the business needs and strategic goals, and must as well be coordinated across functions and levels.

IT Implementation includes the technical design, construction, and activation of system functions in order to ensure that business processes are supported in the best way possible. Input comes largely from the process dimension, in the form of functionality requirements to the system. Conversely, the IT implementation will also set up possible functionality alternatives based on standard functions, which require decisions from the process dimension.

The project will generate changes in existing business processes and systems. These adjustments will mean that employees and business partners will need to learn new ways of working. The goal of ***Change Management*** is to ensure the most flexible adjustment between the "old" and the "new" ways of working, as well as to keep involved parties informed throughout the process. The assignment is very dependent upon which type and degree of change is involved. In the case of small process adjustment, such as learning new screen interfaces, the need for change management will be less than if the change process includes large-scale rearranging of processes and thereby the everyday workload. In the latter situation, the need can range from an employee group following an educational programme, to the transfer or reduction of employees.

The change management dimension receives input from both the IT implementation and the process dimension. Based on these stimuli, it becomes possible to plan which activities are necessary for the success of the project.

It is difficult to choose which point of entry is best. This evaluation depends on the individual company's IT readiness and culture. A main criterion for the successful implementation of an IT system, regardless of point of entry, is that the management has made it clear which goals and objectives are related to the IT implementation, and is willing to make the organisational decisions that are necessary for successful implementation as well as the realisation of the expected process improvements.

Case: Carlsberg Denmark A/S – Implementation of SAP APO

Carlsberg Denmark A/S was founded in 1847 by J.C. Jacobsen, and is today a subsidiary of Carlsberg Breweries A/S, which is one of world's managing breweries. The Carlsberg and Tuborg brands are both among the fastest growing and most geographically widespread in the world, being produced in more than 47 countries, and sold on more than 150 markets. Other subsidiaries and brands of Carlsberg Breweries A/S include Pripps, Ringnes and Tetley's. 95% of the sales takes place outside Denmark.

Carlsberg Denmark A/S produces 5 million HL beer annually and employs 2000 people. In addition to brewing, Carlsberg Denmark is the bottler for Coca Cola, and sells factored brands like Minute Maid, and Smirnoff Ice.

Supply Chain characteristics

The internal supply chain consists of two breweries, one soft drink plant, two main distribution terminals and 16 local distribution centres.

The supply chain organisation is responsible for procurement, production, maintenance, quality control and replenishment of terminals and distribution centres. A third party transportation provider carries internal replenishment transportation between locations. The logistics organisation is responsible for warehousing and distribution to customers. The customers are segmented into the retail and HoReCa (Hotel, Restaurants and Catering) market.

Background

The trigger to leverage IT for process improvement was based on three elements:

- IT upgrade: Carlsberg Denmark had already planned an upgrade of the old ERP system in all process areas; human resources, finance/controlling, production planning, plant maintenance, quality management, sales, logistics etc.
- Supply chain vision: The supply chain vision comprised the strategies; "demand-driven supply chain" and "optimal economic sourcing", which were not supported in the existing ERP solution
- Business case: A previous analysis (1999) of the supply chain, pointed out potential benefits of implementing an APS system to support the supply chain planning processes

Based on the above elements it was decided to implement an APS tool and remodel the business processes for supply chain planning as part of the IT upgrade.

The existing IT platform was based on SAP, and the APS tool SAP APO was already in use for demand planning of beer. Combined with the fact that the company had a strategy of using SAP, it was decided to extend the use of SAP APO for the rest of the planning processes.

Process scope

The IT upgrade project covered the full business model, and based on a business case it was decided which processes should be remodelled in the APS system.

As shown in the picture below the new planning processes was driven by the sales demand in the monthly, weekly and daily cycles.

Three processes were selected as the primary focus during the project, based on their contribution to the benefit potential:

- Demand Planning
- Supply Planning
- Deployment

Demand Planning

The demand planning process had been implemented in APO the year before for the beer division. This first IT project was used to enhance the forecast methodology from manual estimation to statistical calculation based on sales history. The IT upgrade was used to extend that solution to cover the forecasting of the soft drink division.

The soft drink market is highly based on campaigns that could be modelled on and integrated with the base forecasting in the APS tool. The ERP system was not able to support this process integration.

At the same time, the coordination between the sales and the supply chain organisation was enhanced and tracking forecast accuracy was introduced.

The sales forecast is the primary input for both production planning and internal replenishment planning and accuracy is the key performance indicator of the quality of the process.

Supply Planning

Improving the supply planning process with APS instead of supporting it with ERP had two primary advantages:

- Online integration with the ERP system would ensure that actual sales orders were balanced with forecasted demands, thereby incorporating unexpected sales automatically into the production plan
- Network planning based on mathematical algorithms would allocate production volumes to the cheapest possible location and production line based on operational costs for capacity, storage and transportation and balance them with agreed service levels in the sales organisation

Both elements represent major changes in relation to the existing planning process, which was carried out manually. This process did not allow time for dynamic sourcing evaluation, but rather had to focus on completing a feasible plan on time.

In order to support the new process the organisation made the change from local to central planning.

Deployment planning

Allocation of available supply from central terminals to depots was changed from manual calculations to automatically calculated proposals. The existing allocation rules were built into the system, instead of being known only to a few persons.

That made the process much more flexible and efficient, since the planning tasks could be rotated between supply planning and deployment planning.

Project experiences

The project was structured in teams for each process area: sales, logistics, supply chain etc. Each team was lead by the business process owner and comprised members of the user organisation and the IT support organisation, with contributions from external consultants.

Even though the project was organised to address the three critical dimensions of IT, process and organisation, it took an additional year after the project had gone live before the process improvement was visible in day-to-day work.

When the new system went live, it had quite a negative impact on the delivery performance of Carlsberg Denmark A/S and caused a lot of frustration among all involved parties, including the customers.

The IT system was not mature and because of its many errors it caused additional confusion and cost many extra hours in producing the desired planning results. In addition, the lack of alignment between the technical system capabilities and the daily operational tasks required a great deal of manual work to adjust and finalise proposed plans for the system.

After the first critical go live period of stabilising the system, the alignment work between the technical capabilities and processes was initiated. Each process area was revisited to assess the primary objective and then model the planning parameters to support these objectives. The task involved all business users and the IT support organization. Step by step the organization developed the skills and the awareness necessary to operate and support an advanced planning system.

If more time had been allocated to this alignment task in the beginning of the project, most of the trouble could have been avoided.

However, as the processes became fine-tuned, the improvements began to materialise and become visible. Today, the processes are much more transparent and form a solid platform for further process improvement initiatives. The platform serves as a template for Carlsberg subsidiaries around the world, which are implementing SAP. www.carlsberg.com

The Internet and SCM

Electronic SCM or e-SCM is basically the use of information and communication technology both internally and externally in the supply chain, with the goal of ensuring on-line, real-time information exchange between parties. Electronic SCM makes extensive use of the Internet, but intranet, extranet, barcode systems, and electronic media are also utilised.

E-SCM is an extension of the SCM concept including, on the technical side, the business processes between parties, which to the greatest possible extent occur via electronic networks. Sharing of information and applications are also important characteristics of e-SCM. The most important changes occur, however, on the business side, where information technology improves communication between parties, allowing shared planning and control, while giving direct access to interaction with the customer and their individual needs and wishes.

A number of companies already incorporate an electronic element, for example, in the form of order transfers via EDI/Internet, purchasing through electronic marketplaces and Internet sales to customers. However, few companies base their work on an electronic platform and have integrated their information and planning systems with the different links in their supply chain, from customer to vendor.

Supply chain integration electronically connects the individual company with its network of suppliers, transporters, and customers. The point is to utilise shared forecast data, production plans, customer orders, and inventory status, in short data which influences the total supply chain's efficiency and flexibility. The goal is to align supply and demand. Transparency throughout the supply chain, based on real-time information, is a prerequisite for companies being able to act proactively rather than reactively in relation to the link closest to them in the supply chain.

From EDI to the Internet

Until just a few years ago EDI was the most widely accepted platform for the transformation of on-line information about transactions in a standardised format between companies, for example, purchasing orders, invoices, order confirmations, payment transfers, transport bookings, and inventory status. The implementation of EDI connections is, however, relatively costly and assumes that the transmission of large amounts of standardised transactions is profitable. EDI solutions are tailor-made, though, to specific business relationships. The initial investment is as a result high and is lost completely if the business relationship dissolves. An additional factor is that EDI can only transfer statistical transaction data, not real-time information such as actual production, actual inventory, or actual demand. Finally, EDI has a hierarchical structure with a one-to-several architecture, typically involving one dominant company in the supply chain, which develops EDI connections to its strategic partners. In smaller companies, EDI would normally only be used if it was required by important customers. Within the grocery industry, where there are large quantities of daily transaction data, EDI is widely used.

The Internet has supplied a business platform that combines the best of the earlier existing platforms. Like EDI, the Internet facilitates structured communication. At the same time, barriers to access are low, creating no hindrances to small companies using the Internet as a business platform. Prices for software programmes that can integrate external data transfer with the company's back-office solution are falling drastically. Data transmission via the Internet is increasingly standardised as XML-files (eXtensible Markup Language). The Internet can, unlike EDI, support a many-to-many configuration of a supply network.

Electronic Purchasing

Electronic purchasing refers to an automatisation of the purchasing process between a company and its suppliers. The goal is typically to reduce purchasing administration and realise better possibilities for comparison of price and quality between vendors.

Electronic purchasing is most widely used in conjunction with indirect products and services, that is to say, areas of purchasing that are not directly related to production. These areas are referred to as MRO products (Maintenance, Repair, and Operations). Examples of indirect purchasing include furniture, office articles, tools, gifts, travel, and IT equipment. These purchases often represent a relatively large proportion of a company's purchasing total. The individual purchase order is typically rather small, but occurs frequently. The transaction costs and time used in the purchasing of these goods and services are relatively large. In addition, these purchases are often made decentrally throughout the company: everyone is an "expert" at purchasing, and the different buyers have their own favourite suppliers. The potential for setting up a beneficial framework agreement is undermined by the described state of affairs.

The principle behind a buyer-controlled marketplace is that the selected vendor catalogues are converted to standardised buyer specific catalogues, which make it possible for buyers to compare suppliers. Access to the catalogues is gained through a normal Internet browser, which is supported by user-friendly software. This situation allows purchasers to perform most purchasing transactions with little training.

The greatest barrier to purchasing via an internal electronic marketplace is the large amount of work involved in standardising and digitalising different suppliers' catalogues so that they are comparable. This process involves converting vendors' distinct product specifications and product numeration to a shared standard. The cost involved in this conversion process must be weighed up against the potential savings from having established such a system. For large companies that place thousands of purchasing orders a year, the initial savings can be great. The advantage of a buyer controlled marketplace is that the purchaser has complete control over the way the catalogues and business processes are arranged. This aspect makes it easier for the company to integrate the purchasing process with the company's ERP system, and to compare price and quality between suppliers. On the other hand, this process demands extensive start-up and maintenance resources.

Novozymes A/S[23] decided in 2001 to implement an electronic purchasing system to support the acquisition of indirect products. Purchase of non-strategic goods such as office supplies and laboratory articles amounts to several millions DKK, and the number of transactions is quite large due to the relative small size of orders, which translates to disproportionate transaction costs. At the same time, Novozymes wished to obtain a better overview of the entire purchasing process as well as to ensure that buying was done for the prices negotiated in the framework agreements.

From the beginning, the purchasing management was very aware of getting the users to understand the electronic purchasing process. Due to this enthusiasm, interested parties and future users were involved quite early in the project. There was also a continuous supply of information sent out to the entire organisation concerning the project

---

[23] Novozymes is the biotech-based world manager in enzymes and microorganisms with a turnover of 800 mill. Euro and 4.000 employees. www.novozymes.com

and its purpose. Novozymes also chose to allow all users to train by using the web-based training system, which also functions as a follow-up electronic reference system for the users.

The IT solution Novozymes chose to implement was a standard SAP ERP 2.0C solution to support the electronic purchasing process. In regard to cataloguing, the system that the Novo Group was using at the time, which could accommodate 500,000 product numbers, was selected. Novozymes was not interested, at the time, in attending to the development and maintenance of purchasing catalogues, as the catalogues were deemed to cover the purchasing need, and a time period for gathering data on Novozymes' concrete needs and wishes was desired.

In 2003, Novozymes chose, after two years of data gathering and analysis, to establish their own catalogue solution. This decision presented the possibility of creating a self-dedicated catalogue, from which a number of catalogue goods that were irrelevant for Novozymes could be eliminated. This sorting would allow Novozymes to steer their purchasing in the desired direction. There was also a need to redesign the entire logistics flow around indirect goods as well as services, also creating harmony with the specific needs of the business.

This process resulted in the outsourcing of post and distribution tasks to companies with key competences in these areas. On the whole, significant savings in the entire flow were achieved, as well as an increased level of service in relation to deliveries to the company in Denmark, which has approximately 2000 employees.

In 2004 the company was involved with the third generation of indirect purchasing solutions in response to a certain desire for further improvements in the existing flow, through, for example, electronic invoicing, which focuses in part on regional and international synergies for indirect purchasing.

Ken Friis, Senior Director, Executive Buying, Novozymes A/S:

Three and a half months after the project was started, there were 850 users actively making purchases using the new electronic purchasing portal.

Electronic Marketplaces

Electronic marketplaces[24] are Internet sites where buyers and sellers meet to exchange information and make business transactions. There are a wide variety of e-marketplaces.

Some are *vertically* organised and focus on the purchasing of branch specific products, such as chemicals, plastics, paper, and electronics. Examples of vertical marketplaces include ChemConnect, e-chemicals, steel.com, aeroXchange, and Covisint.

Other marketplaces are *horisontally* organised and comprise a wide range of products. Horisontal marketplaces are also referred to as functional marketplaces because they focus on specific functions, such as purchasing and logistics throughout different industries. Some examples of horisontal marketplaces include: transora and globalnetXchange, which are marketplaces offering an extensive variety of consumer goods.

Electronic marketplaces can also be classified as buyer controlled, seller controlled, or neutral. A buyer-controlled marketplace can be set up by a single large company or as a cooperative collaboration between several large companies, with the goal of cutting down on transaction costs connected with purchasing by gaining large-scale benefits. A well-known example of a buyer controlled marketplace is Covisint (www.covisint.com), which has been established by GM, Ford, and DaimlerChrysler, who were later joined by, among others, Renault and Nissan.

Seller controlled marketplaces are a result of cooperation between vendors, who establish a shared catalogue, product information, and available services, with the goal of contacting a broad range of customers. Examples include: Steel.com and Build-Online.com. A marketplace may also be controlled by an individual supplier, for example, Compaq (www.compaq.com) and Nordisk Solar (www.solardis.com). This form of marketplace is referred to as a "webshop." The advantage for the vendor is that the catalogue already exists and that the purchasing portal can be integrated with other information systems and available services. The disadvantage for the buyer is that they lose the ability to directly compare different suppliers.

Buyer and seller controlled marketplaces are also referred to as "private exchanges." The advantage of these marketplaces is first and

---

[24] Based on Skjoett-Larsen et al (2003b)

foremost that they can be tailor-made to fit the company in question and their cooperative partners' needs. For example, an advanced planning tool may be included in order to optimise the business processes between parties in a supply chain.

Neutral marketplaces (public exchanges) are run by an independent third party, who has the goal of creating a marketplace where buyers and sellers can meet. Neutral marketplaces will normally be open to all company sizes, and there are no large costs connected with being a member. Well known examples of neutral marketplaces within the staples market are Transora (www.transora.com) and GlobalnetXchange (GNX).

An example of a buyer-controlled marketplace that is in principle open to all, is IBX, which is owned by, among others, the Swedish bank SEB, Ericsson, Volvo, and Novo Nordisk. IBX is based on a SAP platform and catalogue software from Commerce One.

Electronic marketplaces were initially established to increase the efficiency of purchasing transactions and to ensure greater transparency between supply and demand. Gradually, as the marketplaces have developed, they have begun to offer a number of supplemental services to participants. For example, several marketplaces offer consulting assistance in redesigning customers' supply chains, for example, by offering support in connection with the use of shared planning systems, in choosing and dealing with vendors through the Internet, and in using catalogue services and third party logistics services.

Transactions supported by Electronic Markets

Electronic markets facilitate the exchange of goods, information, and services, and the payments associated with them, but they do not necessarily allow all types of transactions. Four phases of transactions can be identified: *information, negotiation, settlement,* and *after sales*.

In the *information phase*, buyers identify and evaluate their needs as well as possible ways to meet these needs. At the same time, sellers arrange to provide their goods and identify potential customers. To a large extent, these steps orbit around the exchange of information. The information phase ends for a market participant with the submission of an offer. When an offer is received, the second phase is initiated, the *negotiation phase*. Potential buyers and sellers negotiate the terms of the intended transaction by jointly identifying possible solutions, with the goal of reaching a consensus. The result is a legally binding contract, which represents the agreement between the market partners.

In the *settlement phase*, the terms agreed upon are fulfilled. Depending on the type of negotiated product or service, as well as on the participating partners, the settlement phase can be an initiator of logistical, financial, or other transactions. The outcome of this phase is the fulfilment of the contract. A fourth phase can be added, namely the *after-sales phase*, which includes after-sales product support, customer service, and the evaluation of the transaction's outcome. Most electronic marketplaces refer only to specific phases, which support, for example, only the information and the negotiation phase, or the settlement and after-sales phases. However, some electronic marketplaces, such as ChemConnect, try to widen their services to facilitate all phases. One of the most advanced electronic marketplaces seems to be the Transora marketplace, which facilitates collaborative planning, and forecasting, transportation and logistics, as well as inventory management.

The Changing Character of Supply Chain Relations

The nature of buyer-supplier relationships has undergone dramatic changes during the last few decades. Industry observers and researchers have described these emerging relationships as strategic partnerships or "voice relations", as opposed to the traditional "arm's length" type of relations. Ellram (1990) has defined a strategic partnership between a purchasing firm and a supplier as "a mutual, ongoing relationship involving a commitment over an extended time period, and a sharing of information and the risks and rewards of the relationship." It has been observed that partnership agreements are unique for each relationship. However, most strategic supplier partnering efforts share some common characteristics: (1) an increased emphasis on quality, (2) cooperation on cost reduction programmes and continuous improvements, (3) the exchange of information and open communication, and (4) a long-term approach, including the sharing of risks and rewards generated by the relationship.

Consequences for Supply Chain Management

The use of electronic marketplaces as a medium for presenting product catalogues has made it possible to compare product specifications and prices across supplier markets. The buyer will often use an e-market with reverse auction and negotiated contract facilities to evaluate and choose suppliers of goods and services. The focus is on price reduction and the establishment of frame contracts with chosen suppliers. The time period of contracts will be short and supplier loyalty low. It is expected that the use of e-marketplaces for this kind of purchasing will reduce transaction costs for searching, selecting and negotiating contracts with suppliers.

Voice relations are characterised by medium or high asset specificity and can be considered as complementary to the buying firm's core competences. The products purchased have relatively high strategic importance for the buyer. The suppliers will be granted preferential treatment for a relatively long period of time. Planning information, such as forecasts and production plans, will be exchanged, making the planning process more reliable and predictable for the supplier, while also making supply more reliable for the customer.

Electronic marketplaces can facilitate the bidding process by reverse auctions, exchanging information, and negotiating contracts with qualified suppliers. However, when it comes to developing the buyer-supplier relationship, supplementary mechanisms are necessary, such as interorganisational teams, realignment of incentives, and continuous improvements. The types of relevant voice situations connected with e-markets are those that facilitate the settlement and after-sales phases. Examples include: collaborate planning, vendor-managed inventory, third party logistics, and joint product development.

Risk of Cannibalising Traditional Distribution Channels

With the emergence of innovative and successful Internet companies such as Amazon, Dell, and Cisco in 90s, traditional companies were forced to assess how they should tackle the new market situation. The question was not whether or not one should use the Internet, but rather how one should make use of the Internet. One of the main problems for many companies was that they had existing distribution channels that they needed to take into consideration. Would the Internet cause channel conflicts with their other cooperative partners? Would the Internet lead to an expansion of the market, thereby creating increased sales, or would there be a cannibalising of the other existing sales channels? Should a company separate the Internet sales channel from the other distribution channels or could the Internet simply complement and create synergy with these other channels?

In 1999, LEGO Company launched LEGO Direct, which involved the complete segregation of Internet sales from LEGO Company's traditional organisation and sales channels. A project organisation was developed with a group of employees with different backgrounds and experience. The four people involved were free to draw on existing administrative systems and procedures or to develop new systems and procedures. The project was referred to as a "green field" project. LEGO Company chose this organisational form in order to get started quickly without being tied down to administrative routines in the already existing LEGO Company organisation. Agility and quick decision processes are important in the start-up phase because the competitive situation within electronic trading changes quite rapidly. New players enter the market, new concepts are developed, and the lifespan of ideas is short.

It was decided that Internet sales should be kept completely separate from existing sales channels in all of the following categories: sales administration, packaging, distribution, and marketing. Internet sales are organised under LEGO Direct, which already had the responsibility for catalogue sales of LEGO products. In order to minimise the channel conflicts, the prices for products offered on LEGO.com were established as the recommended retail prices plus shipping costs. As a result, it was more expensive to purchase products over the Internet. Moreover, the decision was made to supplement the product selection with varieties that were not easy to handle through traditional sales channels, such as large sculptures and the customised LEGO Mosaic, as well as technologically advanced products, such as Mindstorms and Spybotics.
www.LEGO.com

6. Performance Measurement in Supply Chains

Throughout the book examples of potential for improvements have been presented, and the savings potential of interdisciplinary cooperation in supply chains has been indicated. However, the issue of savings is not the only factor requiring study. Cooperation in the supply chain can increase the bottom line profit as much by improving the delivery performance and service as by reducing logistics costs.

The perception that there are potential savings connected to SCM cooperation can be traced back to the definition used within logistics. Focus here is on reducing the costs of logistics by, for example, reducing transport, inventory, and order processing costs.

A total cost analysis can illustrate how much SCM cooperation can contribute to overall savings, and as a result, why it is a good idea to focus on costs. However, SCM cooperation should not be seen solely as a cost reduction project. Factors such as improved lead time, fewer out-of-stock-situations and improved quality can just as well contribute to increased value by positively affecting the volume of sales, increasing the price margin, or reducing time to market. These factors can sometimes affect the bottom line result more than simple cost reductions. As a result, there will always be a balancing act between potential revenue and the goal that should be set for supply chain cooperation. For this reason, it is often a good idea to clarify the overall goals and results the company expects to achieve by engaging in SCM cooperation.

Measurement Methods

Before the objectives, focus areas, and goals of cooperation can be articulated, it is necessary for each company to have a clear overview of their own key logistics figures as well as how differing logistical initiatives will affect the company's totally generated value. Few companies have this total overview before embarking on SCM cooperation.

Today, there are a number of models of the connection between logistics performance and the company's total revenue. These models make it easier to evaluate and prioritise different focus areas.

A good starting point would be to get an overview of the company's total costs of logistics. The analysis of the total cost of ownership can create a baseline for measuring internal and external performance in terms of logistics.

Total Cost of ownership (TCO) can be calculated in the following manner:

TCO = Purchase price + Transportation costs + Warehouse costs + Transaction costs (Purchase Orders, Goods Receipt, Invoices) + Quality Control/Claims + Handling of goods + Administration costs/Staff.

The disadvantage of using exclusively the TCO analysis as the basis for decision-making is that there is a risk of making decisions that are optimal from a total cost perspective, but which are not appropriate in relation to the company's total revenue. This scenario is a possibility because, among other reasons, TCO does not include costs generated by assets other than inventory and accounts receivable. How sales, for example, will be affected by an improvement in the focus areas cannot be predicted through TCO alone. Therefore, it is recommended to clearly define SCM performance from a broader perspective.

A model that makes it possible to connect logistic performance with the company's bottom line result is the Economic Value Adding (EVA) model, which is also referred to as the Economic Profit (EP) model. This model allows stakeholder value to be estimated at the present time, and for the expected future return to be included in the estimate. The point is that stakeholders focus more on measuring and calculating value creation than on maintaining value. Therefore, cost of capital is also included in the calculations. The definition of value used in calculating value creation is:

The value of a company is the amount of capital invested, plus a premium or discount equal to the present value of the cash flows created during each future year.

The four general areas in which the company's economic performance can be affected are: revenue, cost, working capital, and fixed assets, as shown in Figure 6.1. The different performances are entered into the model, after which the benefit they contribute to the total EVA for the company can be calculated.

The EVA/EP model creates a basis for documenting the contribution made by logistics of aspects other than cost reductions to the company's total net profit.

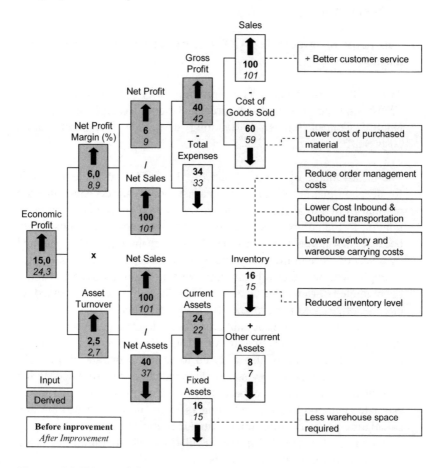

Figure 6.1 EVA model

Some companies have chosen to use the Economic Profit (EP) model as their primary economic management tool. EP is used to formulate long-term strategies, prepare budgets, and to follow up on results. EP is also implemented in daily decision-making in connection with the prioritisation of machines, projects, product development etc. Focus has previously been primarily on production results (operating profit), but today, building costs, product inventory, and machines - the so-called capital costs - are also included, which could lead to alternative decisions about how the company can create economic value for the stakeholders.

In the past, the challenge for logistics was that it could be seen only as a cost that should be reduced to the greatest extent possible. However, by using EP it becomes possible to prioritise, weigh, and balance individual supply chain activities relative to what contributes most to EP.

When the EP model is used, it becomes evident that logistics and supply chain management also can affect the company's revenue through improved delivery performance. This process shifts the focus from only optimising cost effectiveness to also considering how logistics can best support sales through high delivery performance.

Briefly, one can say that the EP model has also become a communication tool for logistics. This model makes it possible for the logistic function to realise management strategies directly through logistics initiatives. Equally important, it becomes possible to make the contribution of logistics visible in the total result.

Measurement Management in Coloplast Logistics

Coloplast[25] develops, markets, and distributes medical devices and services improving the quality of life of people using products related to ostomy, continence treatment, and wound, skin and breast care. Revenue in 2003/04 was 760 million Euro. Coloplast employs 6000 people worldwide and. 98% of the production is exported.

Previously, it was a challenge for the logistics function to draw attention to how its activities contributed to the total bottom line result of the company. Coloplast has chosen to use the Economic Profit (EP) model, as an economic management tool for the use of measuring the value adding of the company. To ensure a link between logistics results and EP measurements Coloplast have developed a simulation tool, there can calculate the effects of changes in the most important logistics areas. In short, the EP model has provided logistics with a communication tool that makes it possible for the logistics function to translate management's strategies into concrete logistics initiatives.

---

[25] Source: Johnny Nielsen, Director Corporate Logistics, Coloplast A/S and www.coloplast.com

Equally as important is the fact that it has become possible to make visible how logistics contributes to affecting total results.

By implementing a new ERP system and Business Intelligence (BI) Coloplast has achieved an overview and transparency in the supply chain, in terms of delivery capacity, inventory levels, cost structures, etc. At the same time, they make it possible to perform detailed ad-hoc analyses and measurements. This has created a basis for being able to monitor measurements right down to each individual customer/goods relation.

The EP model combines with Business Intelligence and an overview of the Total Logistics Costs create a unique opportunity in relation to the formulation of strategies and in day-to-day decision making which over time will create an optimal balance between logistics costs, customer service and capital cost.

Purpose and Goals Related to SCM Cooperation and Processes

In relation to SCM cooperation, the EVA/EP model can also be used to evaluate how different logistics performance affect customer and supplier companies' total EVA/EP. As indicated above, the model can also be used to prioritise future focus areas, and can thereby be used as an input for a business case. The method serves well as a discussion tool both internally in the company and in the supply chain in connection with estimating how potential improvements and results of a closer collaboration can affect EP of individual companies.

Analysing the processes that are integrated in each relationship, as well as understanding how value is created achieves a much better opportunity for adapting and controlling the supply chain. This situation facilitates the prioritisation of focus areas, which will best benefit value generation for all involved parties in the supply chain.

The EVA model for analysing SCM cooperation allows management to increase their understanding of how their company's activities, in conjunction with chosen cooperative partners, contribute to the improvement of the supply chain. This improvement may take the form of total competitive strength and value generation. A minimum result should be the creation of a customer-vendor profitability analysis for each important relationship in the supply chain.

One of the decisive parameters of success in cooperation, both in terms of value and good communication, is that a consensus on goals can be reached. This agreement should include how the goals will be measured, as well as how the results will be followed up on.

By analysing the processes that are integrated in each relationship, as well as by understanding how value is created, the possibility of controlling and adjusting the supply chain is significantly strengthened. Focus areas can further be prioritised so that generation of value is maximised for all parties involved.

The EVA/EP methods can also be used to increase understanding on the part of the management of how closer collaboration in the supply chain contributes to the total competitive strength and creation of value for the entire supply chain.

The effect of implementing CRM (Customer Relationship Management) and SRM (Supplier Relationship Management) processes in the supply chain is illustrated by the EVA model in Figures 6.2 and 6.3. A simplified version of the model helps create an overall perspective of how different improvement initiatives affect the company's total creation of value.

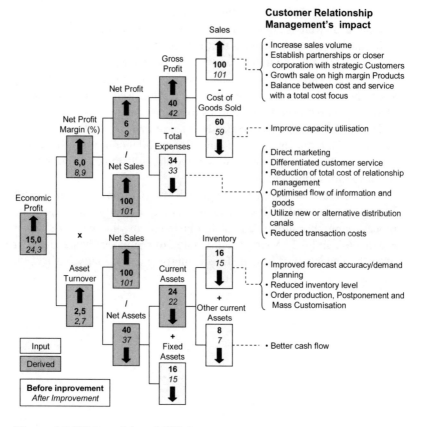

Figure 6.2 EVA model and CRM

In Figure 6.2 a calculation of how different improvements cooperatively achieved through CRM affect the company's value growth. In order to reach a figure that can be incorporated in the model, it is necessary to set up key performance indicators and measure the different improvements.

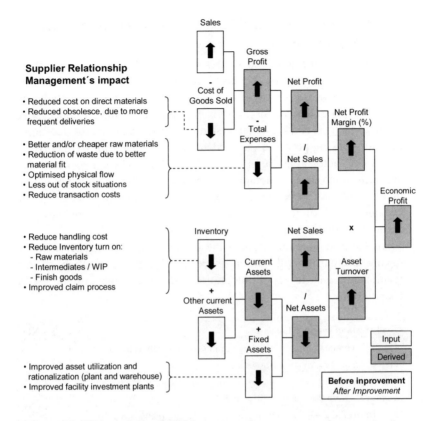

Figure 6.3 EVA model and SRM

Similarly, figure 6.3 illustrates how supplier relationship management (SRM) affects Economic Profit.

If a goal and direction for cooperative effort are not formulated, it becomes impossible to know what efforts should be prioritised. The answers become the same as the ones given to Alice by the Cheshire cat in Alice in Wonderland. When Alice asked, "Would you tell me, please, which way I ought to go from here?" the cat answered, "That depends a good deal on where you want to get to." Alice replied, "I don't much care where." And the cat concluded, logically, "then it doesn't matter which way you go."

Adaptation of Goals and Expectations between Partners in the Supply Chain

Trust between the involved parties is one of the cornerstones of an SCM cooperative effort. Increased understanding and respect for the other's business is one way trust is solidified. This process includes an awareness of a shared mission, vision, and values for all cooperative partners. A total conscious understanding of what motivates decisions, decision-making processes, and what defines success for each party, is also a key factor in an SCM cooperative effort. The expectations that are built up around cooperation are based on these understandings. In other words, by developing an understanding and knowledge of the business areas of the companies involved, a company increases its ability to understand and act based on relevant expectations.

An initial temperature test of the present situation can be taken by having all parties fill out a quick and simple evaluation of the relationship and level of integration they experience in the SCM cooperation.

Evaluation of cooperation	YES/NO
Is there a continual, mutual exchange of information between key employees in the two companies?	
Can employees from different organisational levels speak freely with employees from the other organisation?	
Are the overall goals for a given project formulated totally and clearly communicated to participants from both organisations?	
Is there a constant exchange of both operational and financial data between the two organisations?	
Is forecast data exchanged at least twice a year?	
Is there a yearly evaluation of the total supply chain, with the goal of discussing present and future goals?	
Is there a shared process for reporting and monitoring cooperation, which guarantees continuous feedback to both organisations, and the possibility of making adjustments?	
Are operational goals clearly articulated for both parties? And are these goals used to evaluate the success of the relationship for both parties?	
Is the necessary IT, for example ERP or SRM, implemented to allow for catching and analysing data of key importance to the organisation?	
Does the company's overall culture support an open two-way communication with the selected vendors?	
Total	

The purpose and goal of cooperation, as well as the specific focus areas and goal points are built upon a common understanding of the companies involved. This common understanding includes comprehension of existing cooperation, in addition to increased awareness of each company's mission, vision, values, decisions, decision-making processes, and success criteria.

7. Implementation of the SCM Concept

General Suggestions

In the previous chapters, the SCM concept has been presented via theory and practical examples. It has been emphasised that working in a network, choosing the right cooperation partners, and cooperation structure can increase value in the total supply chain. As a conclusion some general suggestions will be presented in this chapter for how managers and employees can become better prepared to work with the SCM concept, as well as involve themselves in partnerships and SCM projects.

Organisational Challenges

By deciding to use the SCM concept in relation to a company's external partners, management initiates an activity that will entail changes for all employees. Application of the SCM concept implies a different attitude towards customers and vendors. The focus is not on price and cost savings for one's own company, but finding the optimal solution for all parties by utilising the competences available in the total supply chain. This process includes determining which customers and vendors should be in focus through closer cooperation. This closer cooperation increases awareness of the resources spent on each relationship.

The SCM concept is about prioritising and managing a company's relationships. This focus is partially realised by improving the company's processes, through process integration with other companies involved in the SCM cooperative effort. Therefore, in order to maximise the potential in SCM cooperation, it is beneficial for a company's internal organisational structure to be divided up into processes, as discussed in Chapter 4.

Establishing a well-functioning process management is a challenge in itself. Organisational adjustments, the introduction of new forms of management, decision-making patterns, working assignments, and reward systems are some of the modifications that can occur. The organisation often moves from a division based on functions, often with "small kingdoms," to a matrix-like structure, where the functions become integrated into distinct processes. The processes the company's activities are divided up into are selected and defined by management.

It is especially sales and purchasing employees who will be involved in the initial changes. As a result, it is important that these employees are involved in the SCM work, as early on in the process as possible. These staff members will find that their roles change so that they become "anchors," responsible for much of the daily coordination and integration of cooperation between companies. Whereas purchasing and sales were previously connecting links between companies, they become the contacts between the relevant process managers.

Another assignment is to scan possible improvements for processes, which could be relevant for cooperation. Integrating key personnel in the cooperation between companies can be one way of organising this scanning mechanism. This integration must occur through a constructive dialogue with the cooperation partner, in which common improvement projects dominate topics of price, delivery timelines, and quality.

The basic demands of competitive pricing, appropriate timing, amount, and quality are factors to be established and integrated into the system before long-term improvement projects and increased integration of chosen processes are initiated. The message here is that all available energy must be focused on activities that create lasting improvements and shared competitive strength. In order to accomplish this job, the "anchors" must acquire a solid understanding of internal procedures as well as the knowledge employees in other function areas, both internal and external to the company, possess. Figure 7.1 shows the difference between traditional cooperation, often with one-to-one contact, and SCM cooperation, where there are many contact points between employees involved in different processes.

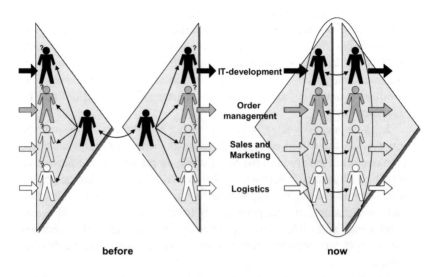

before   now

Figure 7.1 Contact Points Before and After Implementation of SCM

A cross-functional cooperation in the supply chain encourages increased information exchange. It can be difficult to manage this information exchange, as both the number of receivers and transmitters increases. Therefore, it is a good idea to create an outline of the flow of information in a given relationship.

There will often be some departments that react by withholding information and working against internal cooperation. There can be many reasons for this type of reaction. One way of altering this behaviour can include creating goals and reward systems. These systems can motivate cooperation and interdepartmental information exchange, to a much greater extent than is experienced in traditional, functionally divided organisations. Establishing these systems includes developing internal measuring systems that support the desired employee behaviour.[26] The development of these systems can be tackled in much the same manner as measurement methods for external relationships.

Above and beyond the fact that employees' actions should become more process oriented, systems need to be put into place that do not

---

[26] Balanced Scorecard and the Excellence method are examples of possible supporting tools in this situation. Both methods are well known and thoroughly tested in many companies.

increase the manual labour load on the employees involved. The answer is often to utilise IT solutions.[27]

Some companies have already developed a process orientation and have implemented internal systems that manage information exchange throughout the company. These same companies may also have experience with interdisciplinary projects. Companies with the described experience have, of course, a slight advantage, but it will still be a new type of challenge to exchange information with external parties. Certain information will be exchanged with customers or vendors, which would not previously have been exchanged. It is a task in and of itself to find a balance between the basic work of an organisation and the work involved in external interdisciplinary projects. As a result, management should discuss and make clear how large a portion of the individual employee's working day should be spent on external projects and the relationship with selected parties.

SCM Competence

Being a coordinator across departments and companies with different functions, as well as acting as project manager, or even simply a participant in many projects that are developed across traditional boundaries in the supply chain, can often create another type of working day for the employees involved, creating the need for supplementary training. This supplemental training should include information about the goal of the SCM concept, management's vision and goal in implementing the principles of the SCM concept, formulation of goal points, as well as a clarification of, and group work on the topic of working together in project groups with external parties.

The need for and the level of educational training in the SCM concept, as well as the need for actually working with the concept will vary from group to group. The recommendation can be made that the managing individuals who are to function as the motivating power behind the implementation of the concept in the organisation as well as the start-up and follow through of closer cooperation with the chosen business partners, take part in external training courses.

The managers responsible for the above-mentioned activities need a solid understanding of the SCM concept and related tools of analysis. There will likewise be a need for employees in general to broaden their

---

[27] See Chapter 5.

understanding of the internal processes and how the activities behind these processes are interrelated. At the same time, project management and change management will be two relevant focus areas for management involved in the implementation of the SCM concept.

Employees who are to be involved in SCM cooperation and projects must satisfy the prerequisite of being clear about and conscious of the processes of change that are occurring internally in the organisation. The barriers that arise in conjunction with continued improvement achieved through process reforms are often a result of unchanged management and employee behaviours. As a result, the focus should not only be on identifying the improvements, but also on change management and reward systems, which encourage behavioural changes in the desired direction.

It is important to clearly communicate an understanding of the SCM concept, its conditions, and the breadth of implementation the company wishes to engage in. The first stage of this communication process should encompass the employees who will be directly involved in relationships with customers and vendors. Next, the employees who are involved via their role in internal processes as well as those in the organisation at large should be brought into the loop of understanding.

One way of educating employees about the SCM concept is to have the responsible SCM manager teach internal SCM courses in the company/organisation. This method also allows employees performing different functions to share their knowledge with each other, hereby supporting the company's process orientation. The same form can be used during the start-up phase of SCM projects, where there will often be participants in subprojects, who are less aware of the SCM concept, but who nonetheless play a central role in one of the processes important to the companies involved in the SCM cooperation.

The central competences that future participants in SCM projects must develop are the ability and desire to challenge the existing structure and way of doing business in order to generate improvements in the total supply chain through openness, shared understanding of the processes, and mutual respect for the benefit of all involved parties.

Strategic Considerations

The plan to integrate sections of the company's business processes and information at a given level with selected suppliers and customers is a strategic decision. The decision to use the SCM concept as part of the company's business base should include considerations of both internal and external conditions.

Internal conditions, which ought to be taken into consideration when making the decisions described above, raise questions such as:

- *How should the use of the SCM concept benefit the company?* It can, for example, revolve around maintaining strong relationships with strategic customers, creating good cooperation with key suppliers, increasing market shares in chosen strategic segments, increasing earnings, and/or improving capacity utilisation in production and warehouse facilities.

- *How do the visions for application of the SCM concept harmonise with the company's overall strategy?* Here, it can be relevant to discuss the connection between the strategy and the company's relationships to vendors and customers. Does the company's overall attitude represent a willingness to open up to a closer form of cooperation with selected customers and suppliers? If so, what should the selection criteria be?

- *What role should the company assume in the supply chain?* A good exercise is to gather the department managers and totally discuss what role the company should play in the future supply chain. Based on this discussion, it will become possible to determine focus areas, which in turn will lead to improved cooperation and thereby strengthen the role the company can play in the entirety of the supply chain.

- *How ready is the organisation in reality, and what initiatives should be taken and what changes should be made to increase this readiness?* A prerequisite for the SCM concept being able to contribute with the expected benefits is that a reasonable willingness to change exists within the organisation. That is to say, management should be ready to deal with any organisational changes that might prove necessary, and these changes should fit in with the overall strategy for organisational development.

- *How can the SCM concept be implemented internally?* It has been suggested that a responsible party be selected to carry out the implementation of the SCM concept within the organisation. In connection with this suggestion, it should be discussed whether a step-by-step process would be most expeditious in connection with the implementation, or if the entire organisation should be informed simultaneously. One could, for example, choose to focus on the vendor side of the equation, and then move on to the customer side. It is also important to find out who is going to "sell" the concept, and whether or not the right, energetic candidate can be found within the organisation or whether someone needs to be recruited.

External conditions that ought to be considered in conjunction with the start-up phase of SCM cooperation include:

- *Selection of SCM partners.* With whom do we wish to integrate and why? What do we expect to get out of this cooperation? Is it a problem if there are several vendors within the same area? Does it affect the individual vendor's willingness to participate and exchange information?

- *Evaluation of the level of integration.* What level of integration do we desire? Which processes are we interested in integrating? Is there consensus on and fertile soil for integration at the desired level?

- *Formulation of cooperation agreements with shared strategic goals and playing rules.* What are the motivations for entering into this SCM cooperation? What are the individual company's expectations in terms of the results of this cooperation? What are the shared goals? How are gains and risk divided? What is the timeline for this cooperation?

- *Establishing a steering committee.* Who should participate in the steering committee from the participating companies? Is there agreement within the steering committee on the conditions for the project? How can the project organisation be managed?

- *Start-up of project groups, which evaluate the potential for partnership.* Are both parties willing to contribute resources? How will the project group get started? How will the internal marketing of the project be handled? How are the project participants' assignments coupled with the base organisation?

- *Formulation of shared goal points and a measuring system.* What should be measured? How should the measuring take place? Who measures and who reports back? What are the conditions for measuring?

Risks inherent in the SCM Concept

Even though the application or partial application of the principles of the SCM concept presents obvious benefits for many companies, there are also pitfalls to be aware of. It is easy enough to agree upon a reduction of costs of 4-6% yearly, a reduction in turnaround time in production of 20%, an increase in delivery precision of 98%, an increase in sales of 2-4%, a reduction in time-to-market of three months, etc. However, too often details such as clarifying the playing rules, being specific about the individual player's expectations and concerns in relation to the initiative, and in short, testing the "open dialogue," are forgotten. This type of communication, when remembered, can aid in limiting the "blind passes" that can cause problems later on in the course of the SCM cooperation.

Some of the areas that it is important to be aware of before SCM cooperation is initiated include:
- Risk of opportunistic behaviour
- Risk of tying oneself to the wrong partners
- Difficulties in measuring the effectiveness of SCM cooperation
- Problems involved in "fair" distribution of gains and risks

Risk of Opportunistic Behaviour

A large portion of the savings and improvements that can be achieved through the implementation of the SCM concept are realised through openness, trust, and a strong feeling of commitment. Openness and trust create vulnerability, but this is not necessarily an argument against exhibiting them.

The power distribution in the relationship and the risk of opportunistic behaviour are nonetheless conditions that must be considered before one enters into SCM cooperation. As a result, customers and suppliers who have already established a good form of cooperation often enter into SCM cooperative agreements. This good form of cooperation is affirmed through SCM cooperation in much the same way as when people who are engaged get married. But just like marriage, there is no guarantee of eternal fidelity. A SCM cooperative effort does not inherently guarantee that the parties involved will not exhibit opportunistic behaviour at some later point in time.

The risk of opportunistic behaviour can arise in situations where one party suddenly sees the potential for a large gain here and now if they "go it alone," or if one of the parties decides on a crisis plan, which calls for short-term action to correct a poor annual result. The risk of opportunistic behaviour can be reduced through awareness of early behavioural indications, for example, in connection with a specific investment in one of the involved parties, which leads to increased production capacity, or a development project which leads to a contract that ties the other party to a portion of the risk. In such a case, if the other party is uninterested in completing such a contract, there is definitely a sign that there are certain reservations on the part of the party who is taking the risk.

Risk of Lock-in with the Wrong Partners

SCM cooperation, as earlier mentioned, leads to increased integration of several business processes with the chosen partner(s). It is therefore important to undergo a careful analysis, both internally and together with potential cooperative partners, of benefits, drawbacks, possibilities, and potential threats, which can develop in the cooperation, on both the short- and the long term. Entering into SCM cooperation is a strategic decision and should be dealt with accordingly.

Many resources become tied up internally when SCM cooperation begins. A signal is sent to the surrounding world that the company in question has initiated a cooperative agreement with the chosen customer or supplier. A short-term result may be that others choose not to do business with the company. Therefore, it is unfortunate if it later becomes necessary to cease cooperation because of an incorrect choice of partner, or as a result of an error in the development of the cooperation.

In Chapter 2, the meaning of relation analysis is described, and a model is presented, which can be used to help guide management concerning the potential of a cooperative relationship. The central aspects of this model include: gaining an understanding of the possibilities of a potential cooperative relationship, as well as clarifying how well respective companies fit together strategically, in relation to the companies' cultures and attitudes. A "score" results from analysis based on this model, on which the integration level between the respective companies can be defined. It is essential for successful cooperation that expectations and goals are clarified and discussed before the partnership is publicly announced.

Difficulties in Measuring Supply Chain Effectiveness

Management should make it clear that it can be difficult to demonstrate a positive business case through implementation of the SCM concept, increased focus on relationship control, and integrated cooperation in the external supply chain. Discussions will often arise as to how possible it is to achieve the same results in another manner, or with a different approach. For the same reason, it is important to establish a clear purpose and goal for using the SCM concept. However, in order to articulate a purpose and goal, it may first be necessary to thoroughly analyse the current state of the company's supply chain. In other words, sales, purchasing, and possibly production development should all analyse their current relationships, and verbalise their views on future relationships. Based on these strategies, internal purposes and goals can be formulated, which address relationship management and increased integration with the selected parties.

Clarification and visibility of how the company desires to employ the SCM concept create a basis for articulating the purpose and goals related to the chosen cooperation partners. This becomes the foundation for measuring the effect of utilising the SCM concept.[28]

Obtaining a "Fair" Sharing of Gains and Risks

It is not difficult to reach agreement on the notion that it is a good idea to realise savings that can lower prices and increase earnings. Goal points are established for each individual focus area, resources are allocated, and timelines are constructed for the specific improvement projects, lead to a win/win situation from a general perspective.

However, it is not atypical that a company that dominates a cooperative coalition attempts to obtain an uneven amount of the rationalisation benefits. A classic example can be found in GM's earlier purchasing director, the legendary José Lopez, who pressured

---

[28] The method for calculating savings in relation to the company's bottom line can be found in Chapter 6.

sub-suppliers to grant price cuts as a condition for attaining a contract with GM. The same principle is seen in the fast moving consumer goods industry, where large retail chains often dictate the desired reduction in costs as a condition for continued cooperation.

If one does not start by agreeing upon how the term win/win should be understood, then the stage is already set for disappointments and opportunistic behaviour when results are realised. It is not always fair to agree upon a 50/50 sharing of gains. There can be different factors that must be taken into account in determining the best manner of dividing the profits, for example, which resources the different parties have contributed and what risks have been taken.

8. Sanistaal's SCM Partnerships

Sanistaal[29] is a Danish service and knowledge-based wholesaler operating within the following areas of business: plumbing, heating and sanitation, steel, tools and machines. Sanistaal has 1300 employees in 45 industries in Denmark and 16 industries in Germany, Poland and the Baltic states. The company had in 2003 a turnover of 400 mill. Euro.

The extensive customer group of approximately 20,000 customers ranges from one-person companies to the largest industrial companies in Denmark. The majority of Sanistaal's customers make purchases in all of the company's areas of business, a fact which, together with the customer profile, creates a high degree of complexity in the logistics system. The wide range of products with over 90,000 product codes that constitute one of Sanistaal's competitive advantages has meant that the supplier portfolio comprises more than 3,000 suppliers.

Customers' needs vary, and this makes great demands on Sanistaal's product range, service and, not least, cost management in the supply chain. The logistics function therefore represents an important competitive parameter and demonstrates clearly through its strong customer focus the strategy that logistics concepts should be adapted to the different areas of business and selected segments in the areas of business as well as to specific customers within the segments.

Sanistaal has made important improvements in the company's supply chain through a "turn around" of the company's structure, a clear strategy for the development of the logistics function and a number of changes that together have contributed to a considerable increase in efficiency.

In 2001 Sanistaal embarked on a transformation from being a traditional wholesaler to being a knowledge-based, market-oriented service company. Previously, Sanistaal was built up around a decentralised organisation with a number of independent profit centres with great decision-making competence and a low degree of control

---

[29] This case is developed by logistics manager Per Thomsen and project manager Helene Kyvsgaard, Sanistaal.

153

from top management. The area of logistics reflected the decentralised structure and was placed under the control of a number of departmental managers, who in addition to logistics were also responsible for sales and central functions in their own profit centres. A heterogeneous logistics concept resulted, characterised by sub-optimisation in the supply chain.

Between 2001 and 2004 Sanistaal went from having a traditional perspective on logistics to using *proactive logistics*. This concept is based on a clear strategy of strengthening one of Sanistaal's core competences by using logistics as an important competitive parameter. The role and skills of the logistics function have therefore changed from being passive to being active and a driving force in the optimisation of the supply chain with the customer in focus.

In terms of strategy, Sanistaal takes its point of departure in the model shown in figure 8.1. The model shows how each link in the supply chain traditionally has its own business strategy directed at its own market. The companies thereby optimise their own supply chains on the basis of a narrow point of view, which hinders optimisation of a broader segment of the supply chain. A sub-optimisation of the supply chain is thus created.

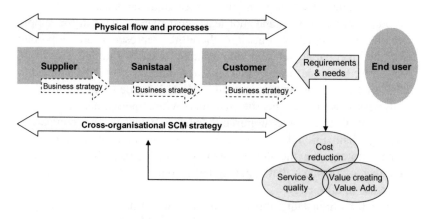

Figure 8.1 Sanistaal's SCM Concept

Sanistaal believes that supply chain solutions should be created on the basis of the companies' strategy and the needs and demands of the end users, resulting in the companies in the supply chain joining together to work out cross-organisational strategies. The joint strategy will reflect the connections between the individual companies' strategies. A strategic fit can thus be achieved between the companies' market strategies and their competences.

For example, the customer company may be highly competent in taking care of reparations and servicing its customers' production facilities, but may lack competences in managing purchasing and spare parts inventory, an area in which Sanistaal is highly competent. There is thus a strategic fit between Sanistaal's and the customer's market strategy.

In practice, SCM cooperation takes its point of departure in "the optimal partnership" (Figure 8.2). Sanistaal operates on the principle that together with the supplier or the customer, it works its way upwards to higher levels as the cooperation between companies develops and the necessary preconditions become available. In Sanistaal's experience, stepwise development is the most realistic path towards increasing integration, as this approach ensures continuous reinforcement and development of the companies' business systems and organisational competences.

How Sanistaal works with SCM

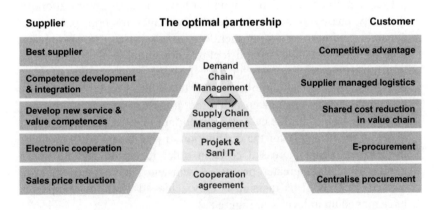

Figure 8.2 Sanistaal's Conception of the Optimal Partnership

Cooperation is based on four phases through which integration and optimisation are gradually developed on the basis of the previous phase.

- Step 1 is a normal trade agreement, in which the price and basic level of service are satisfactory. This means that a foundation exists for the building of trust.
- Step 2: Electronic trade (supplier) – eProcurement (customer). This step means that electronic trade is established and both parties cover their own costs. The advantage for the customer is electronic invoice control and the advantage for the supplier is that orders are received electronically.
- Step 3: Develop new service- and value competences. Joint cost reduction in the value chain. This step depends on customer and supplier needs, but can, for example, involve the implementation of procedures that ensure that an optimal range of goods is maintained.
- Step 4: Competence development and integration – supplier controlled logistics. In this phase, VMI or other forms of integration may be implemented.

In order to be able to ensure gradual development of cooperation it is important that the price of the basic service is agreed upon during the first phase and the price negotiations are kept apart from the subsequent process, so that they do not hinder process optimisation. In the early phases of cooperation, the advantages for both parties are apparent, and barriers do not therefore usually arise. This also means that the parties involved establish close cooperation in these phases, in which trust creates the basis for the expansion of cooperation to other activities. This typically implies greater dependency and the possibility that one party may assume costs in order to ensure savings in the value chain as a whole. In this case, it is important that the parties involved agree on the principle for the distribution of profits and costs if one of the partners bears increased costs in order to ensure that the other partner can attain greater profits. A win-win situation can thus be created. Real SCM partnership is only achieved when the companies have moved up to level 4 in Figure 8.2.

The readiness of the organisation

When a company decides to work according to SCM principles one of the requirements is that information exchange and coordination between functions in the company are high and characterised by process understanding. Moreover, it is important that each individual employee is highly conscious of the fact that his/her work is of crucial importance for the value chain as a whole and therefore for customers' and suppliers' impression of Sanistaal.

The significant changes in Sanistaal's logistics and sales organisation that were carried out between 2001 and 2004 have contributed to ensuring that SCM principles have become a natural and integrated part of Sanistaal's work culture. These changes have made great demands on Sanistaal's ability to change. Sanistaal has not previously had a tradition for large, cross-organisational changes. Primary growth has stemmed from the acquisition of other wholesalers, but even though the companies thus acquired are joined together in Sanistaal, the decentralised structure has characterised the culture of the individual departments far more that a unified Sanistaal culture.

In order to ensure the organisation's understanding of and commitment towards the changes, focus has been placed on three aspects: communication, education and core values.

Many resources have been spent on communication. The primary source of information is the strategy map, and no project is decided upon or carried out without first ensuring its connection to this. Many different media are used in order to transmit information, for example, a new staff magazine, regular information meetings, posters, etc.

A communication strategy has been created at all warehouses, which determines what information is communicated through what media and how often. A regular weekly newsletter has been established at all warehouses, for example, for the communication of day-to-day information. The weekly newsletter also includes the "employee(s) of the week award", which highlights an especially good piece of work by a member or members of staff.

In addition to being a goal management system, Balanced Score Card (BSC) is a regular feature at the regular monthly information meetings. The use of BSC ensures that every department follows the operational measurements, which contribute positively towards the realisation of the strategy. The use of BSC also ensures a very short reaction time from the observation of negative deviations to purposive action.

Moreover, employees have been given courses on the theme "Quality in our Company". The contents of the teaching were based on an understanding of and a commitment towards the changes and challenges that arise in a modern company. The course took place in interplay between information, teaching, workshops and "games."

Since 2001, employee satisfaction analyses have been conducted twice yearly in order to measure attitudes towards and experiences of Sanistaal's values. The analyses are carried out as quantitative measurements supplemented by qualitative interviews, for which the lowest scores are registered. On the basis of the analyses a main theme is selected, which is worked on by a central team while at the same time decentralised work is carried out on improvements in the individual departments. The above-mentioned communication strategy is the result of a project stemming from the satisfaction analyses.

Organisational challenges related to partnerships

When Sanistaal enters into partnerships, it is important that both Sanistaal and the customer/suppliers are aware of the fact that the point of departure is the total costs/profits in the value chain. For the customer there is a great risk of sub-optimisation because the purchasing department often focuses on price rather than the advantages a different delivery pattern can bring. As an example, a purchasing department may, in order to attain a larger discount, make agreements on fewer delivery places or larger amounts of purchases. In some cases this approach may be appropriate from the point of view of the budget as a whole, but it is often difficult for a purchasing organisation to assess the consequences of their decisions on the basis of the information they have available. Therefore, close cooperation internally in the company between the different functions is crucial. An effort is also made in partnerships to ensure that representatives from both purchasing/sales and logistics/production in both companies are included in the steering committee and project group.

A thorough analysis is conducted before Sanistaal establishes a partnership with a customer. The analysis can include phases 1 and 2, that is, advantages and possibilities in terms of purchasing volume and electronic trade as well as opportunities for further development of the cooperation. A more comprehensive logistics analysis can also be made together with the customer, comprising further identification of development potential, strategic considerations, goal management tools and prioritisation. In order to ensure that the customers get an overview and to avoid sub-optimisation, the increased value model below is used to bring to light any increased value potential.

In figure 8.3 is shown an example of the performance improvements obtained by looking at the entire supply chain. The example origins from an SCM collaboration with a large industrial customer.

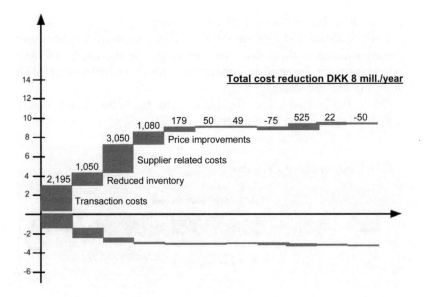

Figure 8.3 Added value in an SCM collaboration

Example of a partnership

As an example of effective supplier cooperation, Sanistaal's cooperation with Grundfos (one of the world's managing producers of pumps) is shown.

Grundfos was chosen as one of several pilot projects that were intended to give Sanistaal greater experience in methods for establishing partnerships with suppliers.

Contact was made between Sanistaal's logistics department and Grundfos' logistics/sales department, after which the project organisation was formed with the participation of the logistics, sales and purchasing functions. The project management was based in the logistics functions and focused on process optimisation. The steering committee comprised top management representatives from both organisations in order to ensure that it had the power to make decisions.

The mutual goals of the cooperation were that both companies wanted to engage in developmental cooperation without any fixed goals. The idea was to initiate a learning process in order to reveal opportunities for optimising cooperation on the basis of process thinking on optimal flow at the lowest possible total costs and providing the best service for the end customer.

Both Sanistaal and Grundfos hope that the experiences they have gained and the methods that were developed in the course of their cooperation can be used in connection with other partnerships with suppliers and customers.

Work was carried out in accordance with the SCM model (Figure 8.4) developed during the partnership.

SCM Cooperative Process

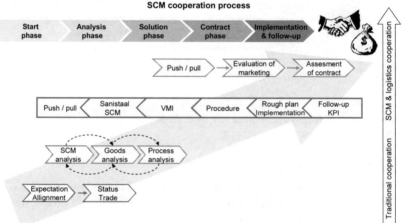

Figure 8.4 Sanistaal's SCM Working Process

The SCM cooperative process comprises several phases:

Start phase
This phase involves the harmonisation of strategy and expectations towards a SCM partnership and the process the parties involved are about to embark upon. The first step is to make an overview of the current trade activity and to sign a letter of intent, so that the parties

involved have formally committed the goal of the cooperation to paper. The goal is communicated to all other parties involved.

Analysis phase

The parties involved develop a joint value chain as a visual and mathematic simulation tool including economic factors of processes and capacity costs of both the supplier and Sanistaal. The value chain extends from the placement of the order to delivery directly to Sanistaal's customer or to Sanistaal's warehouse, including administration, handling, transport etc.

Sanistaal's purchasing of stock goods and special order goods is revealed in a goods analysis in order to see whether the right goods are stocked. Here the push-pull method is applied, which allows Sanistaal's purchasing data to be combined with the supplier's sales data, as this creates the best basis for decision-making. The goods analysis clarifies what goods should possibly be changed from being stock goods to being special order goods and vice versa. However, this will influence costs in the entire value chain, and therefore, before making its final decision about stocking/ordering a group of goods with a given sales pattern, Sanistaal makes use of a simulation model. A clear indication can thereby be obtained of what the joint optimal push/pull split should be for goods in the value chain.

Inexpediencies in terms of administration and operation are identified for both procedures and information flows. The good is followed through logistics in both companies in order to ascertain whether it would be possible to change the way the good is handled so that less time is wasted and drawbacks are eliminated, or whether improved service and quality can be achieved through simple measures. Emphasis is placed on finding both short-term quick hits and long-term benefits through optimisation so that the improvements quickly become apparent to both parties.

Solution phase

Solutions are assessed within the following areas, among others:
- Can synergy be achieved in the distribution between the companies? The supplier is often also a customer, who is visited daily by Sanistaal's vehicles.
- How can synergy be achieved on the basis of the supplier's stock of finished goods and Sanistaal's stock of goods/consumption patterns? An investigation is made into whether the supplier's stock of finished goods and the supplier's geographic location allow the

supplier to ensure Sanistaal's customers day-to-day delivery of certain goods without Sanistaal stocking the good.
- VMI
- A marketing strategy that satisfies both the supplier's and Sanistaal's marketing wishes and close cooperation on campaigns.
- Key Performance Indicators, which can be used both in goal management during the implementation phase and as a follow-up tool in the operation phase.

Contract phase
The normal price agreement is changed to an SCM agreement, in which price is only one of the elements that supports process thinking, but in which KPIs and processes also are important elements.

Goal management has also been crucial for ensuring that joint initiatives have an effect. Some of the Key Performance Indicators used have included:
- Delivery capacity
- Quality of delivery
- Basic data, EDI orders that need to be dealt with manual due to errors in the basic data
- The share of special orders in relation to stock orders (does Sanistaal have the right goods in stock?)

Effects of cooperation
The effects Sanistaal has achieved in relation to its trade with Grundfos include:
- A reduction of approximately 20% in the number of in-stock product codes
- A reduction of approximately 17% in the number of locations of Sanistaal's shops
- A reduction of 7% in the number of warehouse locations of Sanistaal's large warehouses

By combining knowledge of the value chain and market conditions, Sanistaal's programme of stocked goods has been trimmed so that it meets to a higher degree the needs of the customer. This is evident from the fact that the need to place special orders for goods for specific customer orders directly from Grundfos has been reduced because more orders can be delivered from Sanistaal's warehouses.

Furthermore, the procedures implemented have resulted in a more effective and continuous adjustment of stock at Sanistaal and great time savings in the administration of orders at both Grundfos and Sanistaal.

Internally, Sanistaal has also derived great benefit from working with SCM partnerships with suppliers, as the effects and work form have meant that the purchasing organisation is now able to actively include other relevant functions when making purchasing agreements, which optimise the total costs of the process.

A continual process

Today, Sanistaal and Grundfos engage in knowledge exchange and follow-ups on initiatives several times a year. Operations are continuously trimmed, as deviations and possibilities are taken up for discussion during the workday and in the project group if they require major measures. At the same time, VMI is used with the aim of deriving the full benefit of Grundfos' knowledge of Sanistaal's inventory purchases and special order purchases.

Working with SCM has been a positive challenge internally in the companies as it has meant that the logistics and purchasing-/sales interests must be linked and the optimal agreement and flow set-up must be found so that they can support each other. In this respect it is important that everyone is aware of the fact that individual function areas are not sub-optimised. A function is typically assessed on the basis of its own result goals. For example, purchasing is assessed on the basis of price improvements. According to SCM thinking, purchasing is more highly valued if it has contributed to total cost minimisation or improvement of service, which is of greater value for the company as a whole.

In its cooperation with Grundfos, Sanistaal has continuously worked with this challenge both internally and across companies. There is no doubt that the challenges have been many, but the trust between partners has meant that partial solutions have been found. Both companies believe that SCM cooperation is important for ensuring that the companies derive optimal benefit from customer/supplier relations. Cooperation with Grundfos as an SCM partner has been an especially positive experience, as the company, like Sanistaal, places great emphasis on possibilities for development and improvement.

References

Ambeck, K.D. & P. Beyer; *Veje til fornyelsen – Business Process Reengineering.* Copenhagen: Samfundslitteratur, 1999.

Bagchi, K. P. & T. Skjoett-Larsen, Organizational Integration in Supply Chains: A Contingency Approach, *Global Journal of Flexible Systems Management,* Vol. 3, No. 1, pp. 1-10, 2002.

Bowersox, D.J., D.J. Closs & T.P. Stank; *21st Century Logistics: Making Supply Chain Integration a Reality.* Council of Logistics Management, Oak Brook, 2002.

Camuffo, A., P. Romano & A. Vinelli; Back to the Future: Benetton Transforms its Global Network, *MIT Sloan Management Review,* Fall 2001, pp. 46-52, 2001.

CRM håndbogen – fra gruppe til multiindivid, 2001.

Chopra, S. & P. Meindl; *Supply Chain Management, Strategy, Planning, and Operations.* Pearson Prentice Hall, New Jersey, 2004.

Christopher, M.; *Logistics and Supply Chain Management, 3.edition.* Financial Times: Pitman Publishing, London, 2005.

Cooper, M.C., D.M. Lambert, & J.D. Pagh, Supply Chain Management: More than a New Name for Logistics, *International Journal of Logistics Management,* Vol. 8, No. 1, pp. 1-13, 1997.

Daugherty, P. J., T.P. Stank & A.E. Ellinger; Leveraging Logistics/ Distribution Capabilities: The Effect of Logistics Service on Market Share, *Journal of Business Logistics,* Vol. 19, No. 2, pp. 35-51, 1998.

Ellram, M.L.: The Supplier Selection Decision in Strategic Partnerships, *International Journal of Purchasing & Materials Management,* Vol. 26, No. 4, pp. 8-14, 2000.

Fine, C.H.; *Clockspeed,* Little, Brown & Company, London, 1998.

Fisher, M.L.; What is the Right Supply Chain for Your Product?, *Harvard Business Review,* March-April, pp. 105-116, 1997.

Ford, D. (ed.), Understanding Business Markets, 2nd edition, *The Dryden Press*, London, 1997.

Halldorsson, A. & T. Skjoett-Larsen; Developing logistics competencies through third party logistics relationships, *International Journal of Operations & Production Management,* Vol. 24, No. 2, pp. 192-206, 2004.

Handfield, R.B. & E.L. Nichols, Jr.; Sup*ply Chain Redesign. Transforming Supply Chains into Integrated Value Systems.* Financial Times, Prentice Hall, New Jersey, 2002.

Harland, C.M., R.C. Lamming, J.Zheng & T.E. Johnsen; A Taxonomy of Supply Chains, *The Journal of Supply Chain Management,* November, pp. 21-31, 2001.

Lambert, D., M.C. Cooper & J.D. Pagh; Supply Chain Management: Implementation Issues and Research Opportunities, *International Journal of Logistics Management,* Vol. 9, No. 2, pp. 1-19, 1998.

Lambert, D.M. & T.L. Pohlen: Supply Chain Metrics, *International Journal of Logistics Management,* Vol. 12, No. 1, pp. 1-19, 2001.

Lee, H.L.; Creating Value through Supply Chain Integration, *Supply Chain Management Review,* September/October, 2000.

Lee, Hau L., V. Padmanabhan & Seungjin Whang; The Bullwhip Effect in Supply Chains. *Sloan Management Revie,.* Spring, pp. 93-102, 1997.

Nøkkentved, C.; *Supplier Relationship Management.* European SAP Center of Excellence, 1992.

Pagh, J.D. & M.C. Cooper; Supply Chain Postponement and Speculation Strategies: How to choose the right Strategy, *Journal of Business Logistics,* Vol. 19, No. 2, pp. 13-33, 1998.

Simchi-Levi, D., P. Kaminsky, & D. Simchi-Levi; *Designing & Managing the Supply Chain.* McGraw-Hill, Irwin, 2003.

References

Skjoett-Larsen, T., C. Thernoe & C. Andresen; Supply Chain Collaboration: Theoretical Perspectives and Empirical Evidence, *International Journal of Physical Distribution & Logistics Management,* Vol. 33, No. 6, pp. 531-549, 2003a.

Skjøtt-Larsen, T., H. Kotzab & M. Grieger; Electronic Marketplaces and supply chain relationships, *Industrial Marketing Management,* Vol. 32, pp. 199-210, 2003b

Slack, N., S. Champers, & R. Johnston; *Operations Management, 4th edition.* Prentice Hall, New Jersey, 2004.

Stevens, G.C.; Integrating the Supply Chain, *International Journal of Physical Distribution and Materials Management,* Vol. 19, No. 8, pp. 3-8, 1989.

Williamson, O.; *The Mechanisms of Governance.* Oxford University Press, Oxford, 1996.

Williamson, O.; *The Economic Institutions of Capitalism: Firms, Markets, Relational Contracting.* The Free Press, New York, 1985.

Index